THE
SECRET
SIN

LIFELINES FOR RECOVERY SERIES

Can Christians Love Too Much? Margaret J. Rinck

Chaotic Eating, Helen Bray-Garretson and Kaye V. Cook

Christian Men Who Hate Women, Margaret J. Rinck

The Complete Divorce Recovery Handbook, John P. Splinter

Desperate to Be Needed, Janet Ohlemacher

Help for the Post-Abortion Woman, Terri Reisser and Paul Reisser

A House Divided: The Secret Betrayal—Incest, Katherine Edwards

Please Don't Say You Need Me: Biblical Answers for Codependency, Jan Silvious

Please Remind Me How Far I've Come: Reflections for Codependents, Jan Silvious and Carolyn Capp

Post-Abortion Trauma: Nine Steps to Recovery, Jeanette Vought

The Secret Sin: Healing the Wounds of Sexual Addiction, Mark Laaser

Seeing Yourself Through God's Eyes, June Hunt

Turning Fear to Hope: Women Who Have Been Hurt for Love, Holly Wagner Green

Up from the Ashes: How to Survive and Grow Through Personal Crisis, Karl Slaikeu and Steve Lawhead

Zondervan's **Lifelines for Recovery** Series emphasizes healthy, step-by-step approaches for dealing with specific critical issues.

THE
SECRET
SIN

Healing the Wounds of Sexual Addiction

Mark R. Laaser, Ph. D.
Foreword by Patrick Carnes, Ph. D.

ZondervanPublishingHouse

Grand Rapids, Michigan

A Division of HarperCollinsPublishers

The Secret Sin
Copyright © 1992 by Mark Laaser

Requests for information should be addressed to:
Zondervan Publishing House
Grand Rapids, Michigan 49530

Library of Congress Cataloging-in-Publication Data

Laaser, Mark.
 The secret sin : healing the wounds of sexual addiction / Mark
Laaser
  p. cm.
 Includes bibliographical references.
 ISBN 0-310-54911-6 (pbk.)
 1. Sex addicts—Religious life. 2. Sex addiction—Religious
aspects—Christianity. 3. Sex addicts—Rehabilitation. 4. Sex
BV4596.S42L33 1992
241'.66—dc20   91-44404
                                CIP

All names and circumstances have been changed to protect the privacy of the individuals involved.

A percentage of the royalties from this book will be used to aid victims of pastoral sexual abuse.

All Scripture quotations, unless otherwise noted, are taken from the HOLY BIBLE: NEW INTERNATIONAL VERSION® (North American Edition). Copyright © 1973, 1978, 1984, by the International Bible Society. Used by permission of Zondervan Publishing House.

"NIV" and "New International Version" are registered in the United States Patent and Trademark Office by the International Bible Society.

Edited by Dan Runyon
Interior designed by Ann Cherryman
Cover designed by Lecy Design

Printed in the United States of America

92 93 94 95 96 / AM / 10 9 8 7 6 5 4 3 2 1

CONTENTS

Foreword

The Christian church is experiencing tremendous turmoil in the area of sexuality. We have Christian leaders whose sexual behavior has become a problem of credibility for their ministries. They ask forgiveness only to become embroiled in sexual sins again and again. The media exposes their folly, and the sacred becomes the focus of our culture's wit and sarcasm.

The problem seems epidemic. We have a clergyman who has one hundred and sixty-three counts of sexual misconduct with children. We have a bishop whose affair became a national scandal—only to find that the woman has been involved with a series of ministers. We have a denomination facing close to a billion dollars in out-of-court settlements for child sexual abuse. We have a clergyman who preached national crusades against pornography arrested for the production and distribution of child pornography.

The church membership also struggles. Some struggle with inhibited sexual desire. God's desire for their sexual lives remains elusive. The sexual compulsivity of others drives them to a secret life of shame and self-hatred because they cannot live up to their values. Both types probably suffer the aftereffects of sexual abuse, the memories of which reside in the shadowy fringes of their consciousness. So they do not know what troubles them, and even incessant prayer does not take away the pain.

Worse, our entire culture is in sexual crisis. The problems between men and women were highlighted by the nomination of

Clarence Thomas to the Supreme Court. That a whole nation could be so absorbed and conflicted about what is exploitive sexual behavior underlines our sexual pain and uncertainty.

But parents confront this every day. The average age of first intercourse in our country is 16.2 for girls and 15.9 for boys. The vast majority are sexual by the time they are seniors. Parents do not know what to do. They know how poorly the old prohibitions worked for them. Yet in their parental hearts they know how unprepared their children are. All of this is shadowed by the AIDS epidemic, which is transforming our culture. Nothing more clearly connects responsible behavior and sex than this disease. By 1993 we will have over a million Americans infected with the AIDS virus. And with that we sense the emerging awareness of our sexual pain.

The gospel message endures because Christians learn to transform suffering into meaning. Now is the time to focus that healing power on our sexual lives. We have needed voices to witness what sexual grace can mean. Dr. Mark Laaser in this book has done that. *The Secret Sin* is written from the heart, in the context of his own healing. It brings the best of what we know about the disease of sex addiction and challenges the Christian community to face the sexual realities around us. It is a risky book to read if you wish to avoid your sexual self.

Most important, this book places sex in a spiritual context. As alcoholics, compulsive gamblers, and other addicts have found, the path to recovery is spiritual. As many of us who work in health care have found, God does not think in compartments. The Spirit works with medicine and science if we are open to him. Such is the nature of this powerful book. And so should the reading of it be.

Patrick J. Carnes, Ph.D.
The Sexual Dependency Unit
Del Amo Hospital
Torrance, California

Acknowledgments

This book would not have been possible without the strength, help, and support of many people who had faith in me and the project at times when I desperately needed encouragement.

The countless hours it took to write this book would not have been available without the love and patience of my family. My wife, Deb, helped inspire this book in more ways than she knows. What I have written about intimacy was practiced with her. She has modeled to me how to be vulnerable and share feelings. Much of what I "preach" is behavior that she practices. Her encouragement gently prodded me into sharing some of my feelings for the first time. And her forgiveness has shown me that true forgiveness is possible.

My children, Sarah, Jonathan, and Benjamin, have put up with a father who sits and stares blankly into the computer screen. Countless times, they quieted their activities and entertained themselves so that I could write. More than this, they were genuinely interested in the book and often asked how it was going. My prayer for them is this: As they grow in maturity and faith, may the sins of their father not be passed down to the next generation.

In 1987, Pat Carnes was a hero to me, a prophet pointing to the true path of healing. Since then he has become a colleague and friend, and has been a sponsor of my writing. He has been in constant touch, continually reminding me that I have something to say that others need to hear.

Golden Valley Health Center, my employer, has given me time off when I needed to write. Many people there have been patient when I was distracted with this book, chief among them Kevin Brueggeman, a gentle boss. Sarah Fisher, Pat Lair, and Richard Irons have also been sources of support, insight, and encouragement. Much of what I write about treating sexual addiction was learned from the pioneering efforts at Golden Valley. I thank the doctors, counselors, and nurses who work daily at putting people back together. Most of all, Golden Valley has had faith in me and my own recovery as a professional and given me opportunities to teach there and around the country.

Foremost among the many guides to me along my own personal journey have been two gifted counselors, Tom and Maureen Graves. Their ability to confront out of gentleness, to make it safe to discover my own pain, and to show me how to love myself are profound gifts. They have also been models and teachers to me of the process of recovery from all addictions.

What can I say about all my friends in recovery whose companionship was an ever-present help in times of both trouble and joy? For professional reasons, these fellow travelers must remain nameless.

An author is often encouraged by other authors. Writing is more about discipline and less about inspiration than I thought! I am indebted to Jennifer Schneider, Ralph Earle, and Margaret and John Josephson-Rinck for giving me the "push" to get going.

Countless counselors, therapists, and doctors have responded constructively to the ideas in this book.

Likewise, many Christians have given helpful suggestions. I especially thank John Lybarger, Ph.D. and Nils Friberg, Ph.D. for their critique of this work.

The majority of this book was written between the hours of 11 P.M. and 2 A.M. A local Christian radio station, KTIS, has music during those hours called, "A Light in the Night." There were many times of discouragement, frustration, and general "stuckness" when a thought or Scripture on the airwaves saw me through.

I have learned that books aren't written by the author alone. They are rewritten with the help of an editor whose effort gets little credit. Sandy Vander Zicht has been a gentle editor, taking what was often lofty, "fuzzy," or confusing and helping me to make it more intelligible. Thanks to her and to Zondervan for having faith in me.

There Is Hope

Once there was a young pastor who became a full-time individual, marriage, and family counselor. He, his wife, and three children lived in a middle-sized city in a nice neighborhood. The family had many friends and liked where they lived.

In addition to counseling, this pastor preached at a vacant church, taught a course at the local Christian college, and served on the school board. A popular speaker, he spoke for various groups and was frequently interviewed on radio and television. He also enjoyed volunteering for Hospice. All in all, this pastor was well-liked and respected by his community, and many people turned to him for support, advice, and encouragement.

However, this pastor was also a sex addict. He had been masturbating excessively since college days. In graduate school he began visiting X-rated bookstores and massage parlors—a habit that continued into his professional career. Although he was afraid that he would be caught and publicly humiliated, he could not stop from practicing his sexual addictions.

Needless to say, his marriage, which on the surface appeared loving and stable, was very troubled. He and his wife were so busy with family and careers that they had little time for each other. Lacking skills in intimacy and believing that his wife didn't really love him, the pastor thought himself justified in finding a woman who could.

Therefore, when several hurting and vulnerable women in his

counseling practice looked to him for help, he initiated sex with them. He confused sex with love and believed that he really cared for the women, never realizing how much he was hurting them.

Still, the pastor was tormented by doubt. He didn't like himself very much, and he wondered how these women could be attracted to someone like him. Time and time again he vowed to end the affairs, and time and time again he fell into sin.

Finally, a colleague found out about one of these women, and the pastor was fired from his counseling practice. Hurt and disappointed, the colleague and several others confronted the pastor. One of the doctors, a recovering alcoholic, said to the pastor, "You know, your behaviors with sex seem like mine with alcohol. You're out of control. Why don't you let us find you some help?" And he hugged the pastor, for he knew the pain of uncontrollable behaviors.

Shocked and afraid, the pastor was also tired of his double life—tired enough not to resist the effort to find him help. Several days later he entered Golden Valley Health Center's unit for sexual addiction.

In the months to come this pastor discovered the joy and pain of healing. It was filled with childhood memories, the guilt of the behaviors he committed, and anguish over the abuse he perpetrated on others. It was also filled with the joy of being honest, of a new life, and of restored relationships with his wife and friends. He will never counsel or preach from a pulpit again. Several of his clients sued him. Some look at his behaviors with hatred and disdain. Yet, he is discovering the peace of healing and wouldn't trade it for the world.

Saved at the age of sixteen and ordained ten years before he found healing, this pastor always felt unworthy of God's forgiveness. While others admired him, he felt they would hate him if they really knew him. Only in the healing of honesty and recovery has he truly come to know God, redemption, and restoration.

The story of this pastor brings up some basic questions: How can such a basically good person do such terrible sexual things?

How could he have found help before he hurt others? What help is available? Can he be cured? What should be done for those hurt by his behaviors? These are the questions I will try to answer in this book.

Sex addicts, like the pastor, commit a "secret" sin. It is so sinful that almost all are too ashamed to talk about it. Yet their sin threatens our culture and the very core of the Christian church, and is a profound violation of God's law.

The secret sin grows from seeds planted in childhood. In childhood, symptoms may go undetected for years. In adolescence, the course of this disease may be confused with normal sexual development. In adulthood, the disease grows progressively worse. Ultimately, if untreated, its victims will die.

The secret sin is an addictive disease that has existed since the beginning of time, yet it has been misnamed, mistreated, ignored, or completely undiagnosed for centuries. Even though it has killed, humiliated, and wounded countless people, some still believe that it doesn't exist. Its victims have been laughed at, scorned, and persecuted. Too full of shame to ask for help, its victims have been confined to a life of loneliness and isolation. Only recently has the secret sin been named, and treatment offered to its victims.

Christians are not exempt from the disease. Experts speculate that as much as ten percent of the total Christian population is sexually addicted. If true, this means that in a congregation of 500 members, 50 of them are sex addicts. Christians who suffer from this disease have prayed ceaselessly, read the Bible constantly, and consulted with innumerable pastors, but they still can't stop. Discouraged, many leave the church.

Sexual sin is not news to the church. Voices among us have always protested this immorality and called for repentance. Yet sexual sin has always been a difficult topic to talk about. When sexual sin has been committed by "one of us" we are shocked and embarrassed by the apparent hypocrisy and the massive failure of faith. We turn inward to our own shame, fears, and confusion and try to keep the event as quiet as possible.

I believe it is time to bring the problem of sexual sin into the light of public, Christian examination. The church can no longer ignore the problem or imagine that it only exists "out there," for it plagues both our families and our churches. This book is my attempt to examine sexual addiction in the Christian church. We will expose these secret sins to the light of the gospel and our best psychological understanding.

You may think you don't know a sex addict. Sex addicts, however, do not fit the popular stereotypes. They are otherwise gentle and kind. They deeply care for others. To fellow church members they may seem to be ideal Christians. But a secret side of them does evil and harmful things, sexual things, some of them too horrible to fully describe. For some of these sexual sinners, sexual activity has become uncontrollable. They can't stop. They are addicted.

But there is hope. Dr. Patrick Carnes has recognized that this kind of sexual behavior resembles the behavior of alcoholics and that many people are *addicted* to sex. In his classic book, *Out of the Shadows*, Dr. Carnes describes sexual addiction and applies the same kind of treatment that has been keeping alcoholics sober for fifty years. Because of the work of Carnes and others, thousands of sexual addicts have stopped committing sexual sins. They are achieving "sexual sobriety."

There is hope for the church and the many people in it who suffer secretly, or in public humiliation, from sexual sin. There is hope for their spouses, families, and friends. There is hope for countless thousands of people whose faith has been betrayed by the sexual sin of a pastor or someone else. There is hope for those who have been victimized by sexual addiction. There is even hope for those, who, because they found judgment and not help for their sexual sin, have left the church.

I know there is hope, because of the story of the Samaritan woman who met Jesus at the well (John 4). Already married five times, she currently lived with another man who was not her husband. Yet Jesus offered her—a sexual sinner—the living water of salvation. After Jesus healed her, he did not go into the village to preach to the respectable people. But the adulterous woman did. The message of salvation was entrusted to a sexual sinner!

Finally, I know there is hope because I am a recovering sex addict. I am that young pastor I described at the beginning of this introduction. My sin has damaged many people, betrayed the trust of others, and brought difficult consequences to me, including giving up my role as a minister. I, too, have stood at the well in the heat of the day, full of shame, lonely, afraid, and too proud to ask for help. God found me there. Through the help of many, I am learning the peace of being in recovery. It is because of my own desperation that I reach out to others in theirs. I pray that in this book I might show the way to the living water that only God can offer.

Part I

The Secret Sin—Sexual Addiction

1.

Sexual Addiction and Sin

I recently talked with a pastor about the shame of being a sexually addicted Christian. By every indication this pastor is successful. He has developed a large church "full of many gifts of the spirit." Well liked by his people, he preaches wonderful sermons. He is married, has children, and appears to be a normal "family man."

Yet this pastor leads a double life. Many days he is drawn to a local park, where he meets men whose names he does not know and engages in sex with them. Most of these encounters last less than thirty minutes and no words are ever spoken. He then returns to his office feeling more empty than before. Looking for intimacy, he finds instead only frustration and fear. When will someone from his church find out?

This pastor knows he is committing the *sin* of sodomy. He prays, fasts, reads Scripture, and yet he cannot stop. He is alone. Who can he tell? To disclose this behavior would cost his job, family, career, and reputation.

SEXUAL ADDICTION AS A SIN

Sexual addiction is a sickness involving any type of uncontrollable sexual activity. Because the addict can't control his or her sexual behavior, negative consequences eventually result.

Whenever I speak to Christians about sexual addiction I am

always confronted by someone who will ask, "When you call these sexual behaviors an addiction or a disease, aren't you forgetting that they are sinful? People should repent, change their ways, and get right with God."

Let me state clearly that sexually addictive behavior is indeed sinful. But sin, in itself, is also an addiction. Like an addiction, sin is uncontrollable and unmanageable. In fact, God had to sacrifice his only Son simply because we could not "manage" our own lives!

Sexual addiction is about trying to control behaviors—and failing. Just like alcoholics, sex addicts tell themselves that they can "quit tomorrow" if they want to. They like to think they are in control, but they are not. Indeed, their inability to *give up* control is precisely what prevents sex addicts from healing. It is the same with any sin. Our own attempt to control our lives prevents us from trusting God to care for us.

Addiction is also an escape from feelings. Recall the story of the prophet Elijah. After he defeated the priests of Baal on Mt. Carmel he was afraid for his life and hid in a cave. Jonah exhibited similar behavior. So did the disciples in the Garden of Gethsemane. In spite of their experience of God's love and power, people of faith sometimes have a fearful, distrustful nature. This, too, is unmanageable, so they try to escape through addictive behavior.

Addictions, being unmanageable, also lead to destructive consequences. Lives are destroyed, families broken, careers ruined. Sin, too, has its consequences. Romans 6:23 tells us that the wages of sin is death.

Most sexual addicts experience devastating shame and believe that they are totally worthless people. In the Garden of Eden, before Adam and Eve sinned, they were naked and unashamed. After sinning, however, they felt shame. Because we are sons and daughters of Adam and Eve, we also feel shame when we sin.

Therefore, using the word *addiction* helps us define the qualities of sin. To understand sin is to understand more than just a list of sinful behaviors. Sin is the lack of a relationship with God and the destructive behaviors that are committed as a result. Sin is unmanageable and causes people to not trust God, to try to control their own lives, and to commit behaviors destructive to themselves and others. Sin causes us to be ashamed. Sin causes us to die. Unmanageability, escape, shame, and *addiction* are interwoven into the very fabric of sin.

SEXUAL ADDICTION AS A DISEASE

Sexual addiction is also a disease—a situation where something normally healthy becomes unhealthy. Both sexual addiction and diseases have observable symptoms and a natural progression, which if left untreated will get worse and eventually cause a person to die.

Defining sexual addiction as a disease is also consistent with a definition of sin. Sinfulness has a cause. We inherit original sin as children. And sin has symptoms. We don't trust God. We make unhealthy choices. We try to control our own lives. Like disease, sinfulness is also a degenerative process. The Bible continually warns us that we can sink deeper and deeper in a sinful nature. Sinfulness will eventually kill us.

Using the words *addiction* and *disease* gives clarity and deeper meaning to the word *sin*. In accepting that sexual addiction is a disease and a sin, we must also accept that the devil, the power of evil, is at work in sexual addiction. He uses many dynamics to create sexual addiction, including unhealthy families, abuse, and feelings of shame. The devil convinces us that we are evil people. He sows hopelessness and the feeling that we won't get well. There is no question in my mind that we are waging warfare with the devil when we attempt to heal sexual addiction.

"MORAL" SEXUAL SIN

Defining sin as an addiction and disease does not take into account the morality of various sexual activities, for it is not my purpose to theologically define what is sexually sinful. Most behaviors, such as marital infidelity or child abuse, are plainly sinful.

However, there are sexual activities and sexual addicts that, on the surface, appear moral.

Take, for example, the case of the sex addict who never engages in sexual activity with anyone outside of his marriage, yet who engages in sex with his spouse as an *escape* from intimacy, not as an expression of it. On the surface, he is faithful. But God, looking at his heart, discerns his motives.

These "morally correct" sex addicts don't know how to be emotionally or spiritually intimate with their spouse and believe they will find intimacy in sexual contact. Using sex to mask their loneliness, they are unwittingly driven deeper into loneliness, never revealing their feelings. These sex addicts might even say to themselves, "As long as I remain faithful to my spouse and as long as sex is 'good' in our relationship, I don't have a problem and our relationship is good." In fact, the relationship is not good, and the sexual activity becomes addictive as a way to avoid the pain of the poor relationship.

Whether within or outside of marriage, sexual addicts are lonely and isolated. They may have family and friends. They may be active leaders. However, no one really knows them. They haven't told anyone who they are, what they feel, and what they've done. Christian sexual addicts think that if those around them really knew them, they would be hated, shunned, laughed at, or punished. One main question of this book is: Will Christians help to heal, or will they help to increase this shame, loneliness, fear, and woundedness? I believe that in many cases we have "shot our wounded," not healed them.

2.

Building-Block Behaviors
of Sexual Addicts

Fred is an accountant. Each day he sits behind his desk, crunching numbers. But he has more than arithmetic on his mind. Today, for example, he thinks of a pornographic magazine that he picked up at a newsstand. He also spends some time thinking about his secretary, who has been particularly nice to him lately. He begins to fantasize about what it would be like to sleep with her.

Fred exhibits some of the building-block behaviors of a sexual addict. By "building-block behaviors," I mean behaviors that form a foundation upon which other sexual behaviors are built. These behaviors may start very early in the life of the sex addict, even before the child has developed enough physically to experience orgasm. Because these behaviors develop so early and are so basic, they are the hardest forms of sexual addiction to recover from. Building-block behaviors include sexual fantasizing, masturbation, and use of pornography.

SEXUAL FANTASY

The cornerstone for all the building blocks is sexual fantasy—thinking about sex. Normal people think about sex, and fantasy is not unhealthy in itself. Sex addicts, however, think about sex almost constantly. While a normal person might note an attractive person then move on with their activities, sex addicts will not move on.

Instead, they will wonder how they might obtain sex with that person or simply imagine what sex with that person would be like.

Fantasy can involve remembering past sexual encounters, imagining new ones, or planning how to obtain them. Sex addicts do not need pornography to start fantasizing. Any person or event might trigger sexual thoughts. If beauty is in the eye of the beholder, for sex addicts sexual stimulation is in their own eyes. Another person does not need to be wearing something sexually provocative for a sex addict to start thinking sexually about that person. Many "normal" things that any other person might not notice can be pornographically stimulating to a sex addict.

Fantasy might also involve being preoccupied with certain types of people—their appearance, age, status, or personality—or with certain parts of the body. For example, some sex addicts have foot fetishes, and they will fantasize about feet, look at them, and touch them. Other sex addicts, called pedophiles, fantasize about children.

What is it about fantasy that is so addictive? Fantasy by itself can be exciting enough for the addict's body to produce adrenalin, which is stimulating and alters mood. Fantasy can stimulate other chemical reactions in the pleasure centers of the brain that positively alter mood and even have a narcotic-like effect. The addict then uses these effects to escape other feelings, to change negative feelings to positive feelings, and even to reduce stress. For example, many sex addicts will fantasize when they go to bed to put themselves to sleep. Don't underestimate the power of fantasy. Given the chemical changes that it creates in the brain, sex fantasy addicts are, in reality, drug addicts.

By fantasizing, sex addicts are also able to create their own image of a sexual partner, someone who will meet every unfulfilled need that the sex addict ever had. The imagined person can be all-caring, all-attractive, perfectly nurturing, and perfectly sexual. Some addicts will even fantasize about the perfect partner when they are having sex with a real partner, thereby attempting to make that partner into a perfect person.

PORNOGRAPHY

The second building-block behavior of sexual addiction is pornography. Defining pornography can be difficult. If we were to define pornography as anything that displays nudity, then many works in art museums would be pornographic. Yet there are examples of pornography on television shows that display no nudity at all.

Most of us would probably agree that pornography is writing about or displaying in some medium (magazines, videos, TV, movies, strip shows) nudity or sexual activity that excites sexual feelings. Christians might add that pornography excites unhealthy sexual feelings that are immoral and sinful.

Sex addicts can be sexually excited by a wide variety of written and visual stimuli. There can be no doubt that certain magazines, movies, videos, TV shows, books, and strip shows excite most people. They display sexuality in an immoral and unhealthy way and incite sinful sexual passions. On the other hand, a sex addict might be sexually excited by something that no one else would find stimulating. This means that sex addicts must determine what is pornographic for them and not worry about what is pornographic for someone else.

There are sex addicts, for example, who can't watch TV game shows. Almost no one would consider game shows pornographic, yet the attractive models who display the prizes might stimulate a sex addict to fantasize about them. In order to get well, these sex addicts may need to consider even this type of show as pornographic for them and agree not to watch it.

Other sex addicts are attracted to a particular kind of sexual activity, such as bestiality or violent sex. It would be improper here to describe much of this kind of pornography. Perhaps the most tragic of all forms of pornography is that which uses and abuses children.

Some TV shows, writings, and movies don't actually display sexual activity but do teach incorrect information about sex. Consider some of the soap operas and how sexuality and relationships are portrayed. From them we learn twisted models of commitment, intimacy, sexuality, friendship, and faithfulness. We need to recognize that, especially for sex addicts, pornography is more than just the hard-core material that even the Supreme Court would identify as pornography. It starts with the subtle messages that teach us incorrectly about family life, relationships, romance, intimacy, *and* sexuality.

MASTURBATION

Another sexual addiction building block is masturbation. This activity often begins at childhood, when children touch and explore their genital areas. Most people learn from this self-exploration and develop a healthy sense of their bodies. Sex addicts, however, become preoccupied with masturbation.

More than likely, addicts learned early that touching their genital areas felt pleasurable. This may have been the only pleasurable touching that they received. Some sex addicts were never touched in nurturing ways by parents, and touching themselves becomes their only source of nurturance. It might also be that the pleasurable feelings become an escape from painful family chaos. One sex addict told me he got so good at secretly masturbating that as a child he could do it in the middle of the living room with lots of people around.

Masturbating can become such a repetitive problem that addicts will cause physical injury to themselves. An eighty-year-old pastor's wife was admitted to the hospital for surgical repair of lesions in her genital area. Her husband had been physically unable to father children and had become impotent. He refused to discuss this with her and if she ever brought up any feelings of grief about the absence of children or sex in their marriage, he would quote Scripture to her. She masturbated daily for fifty years, and the abrasiveness of that activity had created the lesions.

For some, masturbation is an occasional experience that is nevertheless used to escape feelings or give expression to fantasies. For others, masturbation will take place daily. There are sex addicts who masturbate as many as twenty times a day. The need to masturbate can take so much time it causes addicts to lose valuable work, family, and social time.

A VICIOUS CYCLE

The three building blocks of sexual addiction work together. Fantasy is created by a need to satisfy deep longings. Pornography displays images of how to do that. Masturbation is the physical expression of perhaps the only touching or nurturing that the addict receives. The three of them are involved in a cycle. Pornography stimulates fantasy. Fantasy needs to be expressed. Masturbation allows a "release" of that need.

There is a problem in this cycle. While it may satisfy the physical need for sex, it never satisfies the emotional and spiritual hunger that rests deep in the soul. Addicts have never learned to feed that hunger in a healthy way. Instead, they try to gratify this need in the easiest and most accessible way. Sex at that moment allows the addict to escape and thereby cope *temporarily* with his feelings. The result is that more and more sexual activity is needed to temporarily escape negative feelings. More and more sexual activity, however, also creates more and more negative feelings.

This vicious cycle makes sexual addiction a degenerative process. It gets worse and worse. More and more sex is needed. There are sex addicts who can turn off or slow down their sexual activity for periods of time, but over their entire life sexual activity of some kind will get worse. This is what in alcoholism is called the "tolerance factor." More and more is needed to satisfy the habit.

In sex addiction this tolerance, along with many other factors, may lead the addict to more of the same sexual behavior or to other forms of sexual behaviors. In the following chapter we will examine the other sexual behaviors that a sex addict may engage in.

3

Types of Sexual Addiction

Not every sex addict experiences the same type of sexual addiction. In the last chapter, for example, Fred was addicted to fantasy and pornography, while the pastor's wife was addicted to masturbation. While these behaviors are considered "building-block behaviors," there are other behaviors common to many sex addicts which do not begin as early as do the building-block behaviors. These behaviors may range from the seemingly "normal" sexual encounter with another consenting adult, to illegal and abusive behavior, such as rape or incest.

SEX WITH A CONSENTING PARTNER

Ruth has had sex with at least five hundred men. At any one time she has ongoing relationships with eight men, and on a given day she may have sex with three or four of them. At night she frequents bars to recruit new partners. Looking for the love she never found in her father, she escapes her depression through frequent sexual encounters.

Ruth is a sex addict who engages in sex with consenting partners. While Ruth and many other sex addicts engage in frequent sex with many different partners, there are also sex addicts who have only one affair, of possible long duration, every few years. There are also sexual addicts who have sex with only one partner and sex happens infrequently. This kind of sexual activity may occur between heterosexuals or between homosexuals (sexual addiction can't be *equated* with homosexuality).

Sexual addiction with a consenting partner can be described along a spectrum. At one end are those who have one partner and engage in sex infrequently. At the other end are those who have many partners and engage in sex very frequently. In between are varied numbers of partners and frequencies. The definition of sexual addiction does not depend on where a person falls on the spectrum but on *why* they practice the sexual behavior. Therefore, even if a person has had only one affair, it could be that it was addictive if sex was used to escape feelings, was not an expression of intimacy between the two people, and led to destructive consequences.

For some sex addicts the consenting partner is the spouse. There are married couples who avoid talking to each other by engaging in multiple, daily sexual acts. They may ask their partner to perform types of sexual activity that the partner doesn't like and is even repulsed by. The fact that many of these partners consent is part of their disease of sexual co-addiction. (Co-addiction is discussed further in chapter 12.)

PROSTITUTION

The use of prostitution is very basic to many sex addicts. While prostitution is illegal in most states, the legal consequences are seldom serious. There are also subtle forms of prostitution which are not illegal.

Because prostitution clients pay for sex as if it were a business transaction, they do not need to get involved with people like they might have to if they were to begin an affair. Some addicts might even justify it in their minds on the assumption that "No one is getting hurt."

Today we have massage parlors, "escort" services, and "modeling" agencies to go along with the traditional "hookers" on the street. For the right price, prostitutes will even come to your home. Bookstores and bars feature various forms of nude dancing, and often those dancers or models will engage in prostitution.

One popular form of prostitution occurs today over the telephone. Late-night television advertises 900-numbers that you can call to "discuss" various sexual activities. Even this kind of promotion recognizes the nature of sexual addiction, appealing not only to erotic needs but also to the deep need for connection to another human being. In these commercials an attractive woman talks about loneliness, friendship, connection, and intimacy. Sex addicts spend small fortunes on prostitution, just like the alcoholic who drinks away his paycheck. At our hospital, we treat sex addicts who have spent thousands of dollars on these phone services.

Prostitution also appeals to the fantasizing nature of the sex addict. In the movie *Pretty Woman*, for example, when Richard Gere asks Julia Roberts, who plays a prostitute, what her name is, she replies, "What would you like it to be?" She knows many of her "customers" have elaborate fantasies of who or what they want her to be. Prostitution can play upon the fantasizing of the sex addict.

Sex addicts may get more kindness and nurturing from a prostitute than they ever did from someone else. One sex addict loves to be diapered by prostitutes. He gets powdered, diapered, and cooed over as if he were a baby. With sex addicts and prostitution, we are not just dealing with perverted adults looking to satisfy their lust. We are dealing with babies and young children in adult bodies who are looking for love in all the wrong places.

EXHIBITIONISM AND VOYEURISM

Sexual addiction also takes forms that are not as common and which are illegal. Practicing them might cause sex addicts to be arrested. Exhibitionism and voyeurism are two such activities that involve more than the "flasher" in a raincoat or a "Peeping Tom" at a window.

Mary, for example, owned a certain transparent green blouse that left little to the imagination. She wore it to various bars, not so much to recruit new partners as to watch the reactions of men who saw her. When she aroused them it gave her a sense of control she never had when her father and brothers sexually molested her.

Jay loved to go into clothing stores where the dressing rooms were out in the middle of the store. He would take clothes in them that he never intended to buy and leave the door slightly open waiting for women to come by. He felt a rush of excitement when he saw the surprised looks on their faces. Jay was addicted to his fantasies of those looks and what they might mean. He was also addicted to the adrenalin rush.

Tom, another sex addict, also liked to frequent clothing stores. However, he would loiter in sections that sold women's underwear and pretend to buy something for his wife. Tom stationed himself close to the dressing rooms hoping to catch a glimpse of someone changing.

These are but a few of the endless and creative ways sex addicts might exhibit themselves. "Browsing" in lingerie departments, positioning oneself to get a look when someone bends over, or simply "undressing someone with your eyes" may be forms of voyeurism.

In addition to physical exposure and voyeurism, a person can perform these activities emotionally. Some of these addicts will tell sexual jokes to get a sexual "high." Other addicts are turned on by hearing intimate details of sexual activity. Such addicts may in turn talk about their own sex lives, and hence "exhibit" themselves emotionally. Often this form of sexual addiction is found in the counseling and clergy professions, where it is easy to gain access to the intimate details of people's lives. Not only is this a violation of professional ethics, it can be extremely uncomfortable for the counselee.

INDECENT LIBERTIES

Indecent liberties occur when a person has physical contact of a sexual nature with another person. The other person has not agreed to it and may possibly be unaware that it has happened. Grabbing, pinching, tickling, rubbing up against, and other forms of contact in places such as elevators and grocery stores may constitute an indecent liberty. Even hugs as an expression of caring may have a sexual meaning to the sex addict. A recent graduate of our sexual dependency unit referred to himself as the "hugging priest." He came to the hospital only after several female members of his congregation complained to the bishop about how uncomfortable they felt with his hugs.

OBSCENE PHONE CALLS

This type of sexual activity includes more than the person who talks dirty or breathes heavily on the phone. Rick, for example, was a pastor who called female members of his congregation to talk about church business, and masturbated to the sound of their voice. Another pastor randomly called women out of the phone book and tried to arrange meetings, some of which became sexual.

BESTIALITY

Bestiality, or sexual activity with animals, is another broad category and may involve a variety of acts. Bestiality is a problem in some rural cultures where it may even be perceived as a humorous adolescent rite of passage. Bestiality is certainly not confined to rural areas, however, and there are pornographic materials devoted to this behavior. For example, Larry was a New York City policeman who moonlit for a local veterinarian to satisfy his addiction to sex with large dogs.

RAPE, INCEST, AND CHILD MOLESTING

Finally, there are sexual activities that are clearly exploitative, abusive, and criminal. *Rape, incest,* and *child molesting* are three. Rape occurs when physical force is used to engage a person in sex against his or her will. Incest is sexual activity between members of a biological family, and child molesting is an adult engaging in sex with a dependent child by using physical or emotional force. These forms of sexual activity have serious legal consequences and generally involve prison sentences.

To these three must be added the sexual activity between two adults not biologically related in which one of them is in an authority or power position, such as a doctor, lawyer, teacher, employer, or older adult. This is sometimes referred to as *authority rape*. Even though the person not in power may have said yes or even initiated the sexual activity, the consent or the initiation is not *freely* given because of the influence or emotional power that the other person holds. In these situations the person not in power is the *victim*.

Authority rape assumes that the victim believes the exploiter to be powerful, knowledgeable, or even "sacred." The victim wants to be part of that power, to be nurtured by the authority, and will do anything to accomplish this nurturance. The victim may have been molested as a child, and associates sexual activity with nurturance and people in power. The victim then transfers to the authority a parentlike quality.

Some of these criminal forms of activity may reflect sexual addiction and some may not.[1] Some sex offenders are sociopathic (they don't have a sense of right and wrong), and/or they have other personality disorders. For them, acting out may be expressions of these disorders, of anger and rage, and of a need to punish and control.

In chapter 6 I will discuss the fact that sex addicts are in most cases themselves victims of sexual abuse. The fear and anger that their own abuse created may cause them to abuse others when they grow up. However, saying this does not at all justify this kind of sexual offense.

SUMMARY

In this chapter I have explored a number of activities that a sexual addict may engage in. However, this list is by no means complete. I chose not to describe some of the extremes that can take place.

The most common behaviors are still the building-block behaviors of fantasy, pornography, and masturbation, and some addicts focus on these activities alone. Others who commit more serious forms of sexual addiction may also practice these less serious forms, sometimes as a way of controlling the more severe behaviors.

In the diagnosis of sexual addiction it is important not to focus on the behaviors alone, for it's often easy to get stuck thinking about the immoral, illegal, or bizarre nature of some of them. In addition, sex addicts may excuse their addiction to fantasy or pornography by saying, "I've never raped anyone, so I'm not a sex addict." However, if this person engages in any uncontrollable repetitive sexual behavior, he or she *is* a sexual addict.

Whether sex addicts have committed rape or only fantasized about sex, they will have certain features common to all sex addicts. In the next chapter I will describe these common characteristics.

4.

Characteristics of Sexual Addiction

Ryan is a successful doctor and respected family man. His bedside manner is quick and brusque, but he smiles often and says the right things. A popular man, he has countless friends. But Ryan and his wife generally don't have time for each other, being too distracted by their work, social life, and children.

Lately, after busy days at the hospital, Ryan has been engaging in sex with prostitutes. He also suffers from occasional outbursts of anger at work, but the staff excuses his behavior, saying he is a busy man and the stress of caring for his patients must be great. Everyone around him assumes that since Ryan helps others with their problems, he doesn't have problems himself. They also assume that since people around Ryan like him, Ryan must like himself. But Ryan hates himself, his behaviors, and his work. Being a doctor helps him feel important temporarily, but the feeling wears off. He is beginning to consider suicide.

SELF-IMAGE

Sex addicts like Ryan have a poor self-image. They perceive themselves as bad, evil people. Those around them may not know this, however, because such people may at times act as if they think highly of themselves. They may act with bravado, boast often, promote themselves, or appear self-righteous. They may also seem conceited or obnoxious. Sex addicts who try to convince others of how wonderful they are, actually are trying to convince themselves that they are good people.

Some sex addicts play a martyr role. Their perception that they are bad leads them to believe that the "world" and everyone in it doesn't like them and that bad things will always happen. They may feel that everyone is trying to take advantage of them, and that the only attention they are going to get is sympathy from those who feel sorry for them. Their behavior is extremely frustrating to relatives or friends because they are never happy, won't take or implement constructive advice, and continue to complain even in the face of apparent success.

Sex addicts may be overachievers. However, whatever they might accomplish in life is never good enough to convince them that they are good people. Always looking for the next triumph or accomplishment, they become addicted to the "high" of winning. Some sexually addicted pastors are addicted to applause. But the temporary fix of being complimented on a sermon doesn't last long. By Sunday afternoon the old convictions of innate badness return.

Sex addicts may also be underachievers, never quite living up to their potential. Afraid to risk trying to accomplish something for fear they couldn't do it, they would rather live with the possibility that they could accomplish something if they tried. "If I had wanted to I could have gone to law school and become a lawyer, but it just didn't work out," they may say.

Sex addicts may seem very self-sufficient. One of their basic beliefs is that no one will take care of them because no one loves them as they are. At other times or to other people they may seem very needy, as if they always depend on someone else to take care of them.

The negative self-image of the sex addict leads to chronic depression. The vast majority, seventy-one percent according to Patrick Carnes's research, have thought of suicide.[1] Many have tried. Some have been successful.

MOOD ALTERATION AND ESCAPE

Barry has a hard time sleeping at night. His job is stressful. His children are rebellious. He worries about money, and he and his wife argue continually about the checkbook and the charge cards. He finds himself frequently sneaking off to the bathroom, at home and at work, to masturbate. Now it seems that he can't go to sleep without sex. Since his wife is unwilling most of the time, he either fantasizes or masturbates.

Very early in the life of most sex addicts, sex became a solution to painful situations. The pleasurable feelings of sexuality were perhaps the only relief they knew. Sex became an escape, a way of altering their mood. They felt no one else was doing anything for them, so they took matters into their own hands. Sex was a way of *coping*.

As sex addicts grow up, sex remains a means of coping with stress. When painful feelings occur sex becomes a way to "medicate" that pain. Even fantasy, without a more direct form of sexual contact, can be soothing to a sex addict.

ENTITLEMENT

When there isn't stress, sex can also be seen as a reward. Since sex addicts believe that no one will take care of them and they must do everything for themselves, they begin to build up resentment. While one part of them feels they don't deserve anything and that they are bad people, a deeper and unconscious part of them wants to believe differently. Perhaps this is a very spiritual part, a knowledge of their potential for goodness, a connection to a God who loves them.

Sex addicts, however, don't have a healthy sense of how to reward themselves or how to give themselves affirmation. Their anger and resentment can express itself as a sense of *entitlement*. "I deserve something," they think. After surviving stressful events, performing well, or doing a good job, sex addicts may believe that they deserve to be rewarded sexually.

Perhaps, for example, a sex addict is surviving a bad marriage or a bad job. They stay with it believing this is the moral and faithful thing to do. They do develop the feeling, however, that in order to survive they will need to reward themselves to medicate their feelings of loneliness and isolation. Sex becomes their reward. A sense of entitlement gives sex addicts the belief that they are justified in their sexual behaviors.

UNMANAGEABILITY AND EFFORTS TO CONTROL

A psychiatrist in South Carolina reported to me that he had a patient who was addicted to pornography. This person was a very religious man who read the Bible continually. He tried various methods to stop the pornography addiction, but without success. Finally, he took a biblical injunction seriously and plucked out both eyes because they continued to offend him.

Sexual addicts try to stop but can't. They make promises to themselves and employ a variety of strategies to stop the behavior, much like an alcoholic. Some even injure their genitals or other body parts as a way to prevent their behaviors. Some turn rigidly and desperately to religion to stop their behavior. One alumnus of Golden Valley Health Center was baptized in four different churches in an attempt to take away his sexual desire.

Usually this religious approach leads to frustration, shame, and despair. A sexual addict believes that, "I was bad before. Not even my faith can save me; therefore I must really be a bad person." Often these people turn away from religion altogether. Going to church reminds them of their failure, or they feel God has not loved them enough to take away their lust.

When sex addicts try desperately to control their disease they may succeed for various lengths of time. We call this "acting in" or "white knuckling." Acting in is the opposite of acting out. This is an extremely important phenomenon. Many sex addicts deny they are addicted because they have been acting in or white knuckling for long periods of time. In this form of total self-denial they completely turn off their sexuality.

Acting in may be based on the Christian's fear of God. It is certainly biblical that we fear God in the same sense that we fear parents who love us. We respect their authority and know that, in love, we will be punished as a corrective way to get us back on the path. Although we may not understand it at the time, punishment is for our correction and rehabilitation.

Christian sex addicts may fear God but not have this understanding. They are simply afraid. Acting in may be their way of trying to manipulate God so that he will not punish them. They turn off sexual feelings not to honor God out of healthy fear, but out of an unhealthy fear that God is an angry God.

This phenomenon has many parallels with eating disorders (see figure 1). Anorexics will act in, stopping their eating as an effort to control weight. This is an effort to control their image of their bodies, their lives, and even their sexuality.

This is important for Christians to understand because at times sexual anorexics justify their acting in by their Christian beliefs. They base this behavior on the belief that the body is innately "bad" and that if the spirit can be "freed" from the desires and temptations of the body, a person will be more acceptable to God. Sexual self-denial is seen as highly spiritual behavior.

Sex addicts make repeated efforts in many other ways to turn off their sexual behaviors. Some may try moving, thinking they won't act out in a new environment. For example, churches often transfer pastors who have sexually acted out, thinking that they will not repeat their behaviors because the shame of being found out once again would be too painful. However, this "geographic cure" rarely works. Because sex addicts don't know how to cope with shame and emotional pain in healthy ways, they use sex to cope.

Tragically, sex addicts have often tried to get help by telling someone, but they haven't been believed, heard, or understood. Pastors may have been quick to forgive behaviors or quick to moralize about the need to stop. Psychiatrists and counselors may have excused the sexual behaviors as "normal." Because many

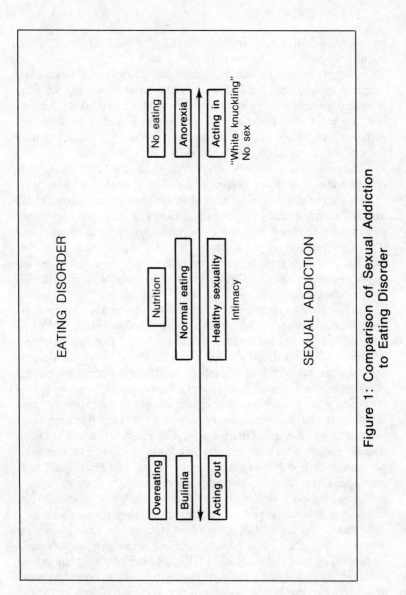

Figure 1: Comparison of Sexual Addiction
to Eating Disorder

therapists want to loosen rigid moral attitudes about sex and increase awareness of the joy of sex, they have not *heard* the pain of sex addicts trying to explain that their sexual activity is uncontrollable. The sex addict, often ignored or misunderstood by his family, now faces the pain of being ignored by those he has turned to for help.

DENIAL AND DELUSIONS

Some sex addicts have never tried to get help, or else have stopped trying. Fear of strong moral judgment or social consequences keeps them silent and alone. They think, "Whom do I tell? Other people will get angry with me, reject me, or go running and screaming out of the room. I will lose my job, my family, my social standing." These fears create a deep need to be silent and an even more desperate need to control the behavior. This fear of negative consequences and rejection, and the resulting need to control becomes intense for any addict. If they are ever confronted with their behaviors they will either *deny* those behaviors or claim they are in control: "If I wanted to, I could quit."

Often addicts will try to justify their behaviors. "I was lonely. My spouse is never sexual with me. People are always taking advantage of me. He seduced me in a weak moment." At other times addicts will lie. "I really didn't do that. Where did you get that information? You are wrong. Are you trying to hurt me?"

One of the tools of denial is *delusion*, the belief that the addictive behavior is not really that bad or harmful. It is hard for an outsider to imagine how convincing sex addicts can be to themselves. We might wonder how a person could commit sinful, immoral, and illegal behaviors. The answer is that they *may* have deluded themselves into thinking their behaviors aren't "that bad," and that they really aren't hurting themselves or anyone else.

People who are in denial or deluding themselves may very well *benefit* from being confronted with their behaviors. Some of them may also need to suffer the consequences of their behavior in order to understand their negative and destructive nature.

TOLERANCE

The alcoholic will build tolerance of alcohol and therefore need more and more alcohol to achieve the same mood-altering effect. A sex addict is no different, needing to act out more and more frequently to obtain the same high.

Terry was a homosexual who frequented relatively safe gay bars in respectable neighborhoods. He made anonymous contacts with men who were gentle like him. This routine became somewhat boring, so he began to visit more dangerous neighborhoods, where he found all sorts of rougher men. These encounters became more physically dangerous. While he was afraid of this, it also excited him.

Part of the addictive quality of sex is that it is exciting, sometimes because it is dangerous. When a given activity becomes routine a sex addict may progress to more dangerous or exciting forms of it. This may be as simple as progressing from masturbating in private to masturbating in more public places, from having affairs with single people to having affairs with married people, or from picking up partners in relatively safe places to finding them in more dangerous places. For some, it may also mean a progression to more illegal forms of sex.

BLACKOUTS

Kevin met a man at a bar. Even though he wanted to watch the World Series at the bar, he went home with this man and engaged in sex with him. Later that evening when he left, he was surprised to hear sirens and people scurrying around. Many lights were out, and chaos reigned. While he had been having sex, San Francisco had experienced one of its most devastating earthquakes, yet he had not felt even the most violent of the tremors.

Alcohol often causes blackouts—the inability to remember what happened. Alcoholics can "wake up" in unfamiliar places and not know how they got there or what happened the night before. Sex addicts, too, experience blackouts when they are intensely involved in what they are doing. They, too, will wake up in strange beds and not know how they got there.

There are several possible reasons for blackouts. Many sex addicts use alcohol, and that causes the blackout. Another possibility is that their experiences are so emotionally painful that their brain naturally and protectively suppresses the memories. Finally, it could be that the denial and delusional mechanisms are so strong that the addict "refuses" to remember.

RIGIDITY AND BLAMING

Phil, a seminary student studying to be a priest, struggled with masturbation and homosexual feelings. His spiritual director advised him that whenever he felt sexual temptation he should say the rosary five times and the temptation would go away. But it didn't work. He searched for other prayers and rituals that might help him, but nothing seemed to help him.

Phil's first parish was a conservative ethnic one in a poor neighborhood. The men there told jokes about homosexual men, and Phil joined in so as not to reveal his own sexual orientation. One night these men began ridiculing and taunting a man who seemed to them to be gay. Then they began to blame homosexuals for all the problems in the world. While Phil disagreed with much of what they said, he too found himself getting angry and critical of the gay community.

One result of sex addicts' desperate attempts to stop is that they may look for formulas to follow. They assume there is a right way and a wrong way to do things. If they could just get the formula right, a list of things to do, then their sexual acting out would stop. This black and white thinking can lead to rigidity. They think there are good people and bad people, good groups and bad groups, and they desperately want to belong to the right side. In the search for the right people and the right side, an addict may become prejudiced against others who don't belong to this group. This leads to anger against those on the "outside." "If it weren't for them, things would be right with me and the world." This is a form of self-righteousness.

Self-righteousness leads to blaming. If there is a "right" way of dong things, there must also be a "wrong" way. Other people, institutions, or events may represent the wrong way and therefore become responsible for the bad things that happen. "It is all *their* fault," a sex addict might say. "If he (or she) hadn't seduced me, I wouldn't have had the affair."

Sex addicts often look to the "right" religious group to take away their lusts. The man who was baptized four times felt he never did find the "right" church. If he had, one of those baptisms would have "worked" and his lust would have been removed. Some Christian addicts believe that God will magically transform them into people who never experience sexual temptation.

CONSEQUENCES

Stan was a pastor who had built up a strong and vital congregation. He had a loving wife and one daughter. They seemed to be a wonderful family. But Stan was addicted to pornography and prostitution. Over the years he squandered thousands of dollars to feed his sexual habits. To pay for his habits, he applied for and received a number of charge cards. Finally, he could no longer pay his bills. His balance on all of these cards was $40,000.

Stan was desperate. How could he tell his wife or his church about these bills? He once worked for a bank and knew how they operated. He bought a cheap hand gun, began robbing banks, and paid his debts. After he robbed his twelfth bank he was caught. This fine pastor is now in federal prison because of his addiction to prostitution.

Sexual addicts routinely run the risk of all kinds of consequences. To some the danger of their activities is part of the "high." They risk AIDS and other infectious diseases. They risk the loss of jobs, career, spouse, friends, and money. They may be arrested, sued, or jailed. Depression, anxiety, and other emotional conditions also result. Often sex addicts get so involved in flurries of activity they become exhausted and burned out. Fatigue and exhaustion in turn lead to a host of physical illnesses and symptoms.

Physical injury is also common. The pastor's wife mentioned earlier masturbated so regularly she needed surgical repair. Suicide is perhaps the ultimate example of a consequence.

Consequences do not stop the addict from acting out. I have known several sex addicts, for example, who have been sexual with persons that they knew had AIDS. This is how desperate an addict will become to obtain his "supply," and it is an example of suicidal thinking.

CODEPENDENCY

Pat was addicted to going to massage parlors. At first he sought encounters with young and very attractive women. Gradually, he started seeking prostitutes who were older, resembling his mother. He also started to realize he wasn't so much interested in the orgasm as he was in the touching. Pat was looking for his mother. Every time he came out of the massage parlor he felt frustrated and cheated, but he kept going back, always looking.

Judy was raised in a very strict Christian home. While her father was occasionally home, he worked a lot, attended many church meetings, and otherwise had little time for Judy. He was strict, often angry, and very critical with her. As she grew up Judy found herself getting attached to one man after another. She desperately needed their approval. She would do anything for them. If this included sex, so be it. Gradually, she found that she needed sex just to feel relaxed or temporarily content. Each man got bored with the relationship and left her. Every time, after intense grieving, she went out and found another. She has been married five times and has had numerous affairs.

Sexual addicts crave the nurturing they have not received. They don't feel worthy of nurturance, but they seek it to fill deep holes in themselves. In looking for this connection they will become attached to people that represent this connection. In so doing they can become totally dependent on these people, a behavior known as codependency. Sex addicts are codependents, addicted to one or more people.

RELATIONSHIPS

Codependency affects how sex addicts relate to all people. They sacrifice themselves and their interests and values in order to please someone else.

Sexual addiction is also an intimacy disorder. Sex addicts are not able to be vulnerable emotionally with other people. They would never tell anyone honestly how they're feeling, for they are probably not aware of how they feel themselves. Generally their feelings are painful and to be avoided at all costs.

Sex addicts have great difficulty, then, relating on a deep personal level with other people. They may lie to cover up their behaviors, delude themselves and others about themselves, and generally lead a double life—one life that everyone knows and the secret life that only they know. These are not factors that create meaningful relationships. The people whom sex addicts are most afraid of losing are the ones the sex addicts are least likely to tell who they really are. They fear that if their loved ones really knew them, they would be rejected and abandoned.

One feature of the double life of sex addicts is their ability to tell some of their feelings to strangers and not be able to talk at all to those close to them. This creates considerable anger for spouses, family members, and others who would like to get closer, can't, and then see their sex addicts opening up to others. But the sex addicts are less afraid of losing the stranger.

The relationships of sex addicts are often stormy and unsuccessful. They may be of a short-term nature and are certainly superficial in depth, even though the sex addict may be very dependent on the partner. This dynamic of codependency is often called "enmeshment." A sex addict may desperately "cling" to someone for love, attention, and approval: "I would die if you left me."

Enmeshment can be very dramatic but it is not deeply

intimate. Sex addicts may be enmeshed with people who need them desperately, allowing them to feel needed. Or they may be enmeshed with people who take care of them, thus allowing them to be irresponsible.

As part of the secret, double life, sex addicts will not like being responsible for time. They will lie about where they've been and whom they've seen. They love "free" time and jobs that don't have regular structure, because it gives them the freedom to "escape" to their addictive activities. They also spend money on themselves and their addictive activity and don't like having to explain where it went. Sex addicts may, in fact, be compulsive spenders for things other than sexual activities.

Sex addicts are "slippery." They may have lots of acquaintances but no friends. They may be the life of the party but no one knows them. They may have wonderful public reputations, but it would shock many to know what they do sexually. They avoid accountability to anyone so that they will have the freedom to pursue their life-style.

Finally, many sex addicts experience what is called "gender hatred," seeming to "hate" all men or all women. Men who sexually act out with women, for example, may be accused of hating women, particularly if the sex is exploitative, abusive, or manipulative. However, sex addicts do not actually hate all men or all women. Rather, they are blaming women or men for abuse suffered in childhood. If a man abused them in early years, any man who comes along later in life may take on the attributes of the original abuser. The anger felt toward the original abuser will be misplaced onto the current person, a process called "projection." Old feelings from old relationships are "projected" onto new people and new relationships.

SEXUALITY

Despite the fact that sex addicts have lots of sexual experiences, they may not know very much about sex. In fact, they may be full of misinformation or lack information entirely. Sex addicts usually grow up in families where the topic of sex is rarely discussed. If sex is discussed in the home, it is usually done in the context of negative messages. They are left to discover what they can from their own experiences or from cultural teaching, which is normally full of misconceptions.

If sex addicts have grown up in a Christian or religious home, the sexual messages they received may have been full of the dangers of sexual immorality. Rarely is the positive, healthy, and spiritual side of sex presented. Sex becomes, then, a very negative and forbidden subject. Combine this negative teaching with the lack of positive teaching and there develops an undercurrent of tension around sexuality. Sex is "forbidden."

There is a certain curiosity and excitement in this forbiddance, a natural and exciting pull that many of us would feel toward something we know little about. In adolescence, as sexual feelings very normally develop, we can become frightened of sensations that are in fact normal. Given our cultural fascination with sexuality, this can be a very confusing time.

If sex addicts were sexually abused as children by a parent or other family member, the most significant connection with that parent or family member was sexual. If parents are supposed to love you, and if parents are sexual with you, the conclusion is that this must be a part of the way they love you. This is delusional thinking, but remember that it is a child doing it. These children may grow up to be sex addicts, thinking that "sex is equal to love."

The experience of sex with a parent is frightening and painful. Sex addicts may come to think that for sex to take place it must be mysterious, evil, uncomfortable, and dangerous. In fact, Dr. Patrick Carnes has said that for a sex addict, "For sex to be good, it has to be bad."

CROSS ADDICTIONS

As a teenager Barry drank alcohol with his friends and to loosen up before a date. As he got older he found that drinking allowed him to be more aggressive with women. This usually got him what he wanted—sex. Even though he got married he continued to have affairs. His drinking progressed.

Barry's wife, who didn't know about the other women, demanded that he stop drinking. So Barry went to treatment for alcoholism and later regularly attended A.A. meetings. Although he stayed sober four years, he continued to have affairs, sometimes with other A.A. members. When he told his A.A. sponsor about his affairs, the man laughed and told Barry to do whatever it took to stop drinking.

Many sex addicts will be addicted to other behaviors and substances. Sex is their primary addictive activity, but there are others. Many of the sex addicts who have come to treatment at Golden Valley Health Center, like Barry, are already recovering alcoholics. They may have experienced many years of sobriety from alcohol. They may even have thought that if they got sober from alcohol and drugs they would stop their sexual activities. Tragically, however, their sexual acting out got worse when they achieved alcoholic sobriety.

Some of our alumni at Golden Valley leave treatment, and while achieving sobriety from sex they find themselves having difficulty with compulsive eating. Many start gaining weight. Others continue to smoke heavily, compulsively spend or gamble money, or watch TV incessantly. The list of other possibilities is endless. I remember talking to one of our alumni who in one month had rented sixty videos, none R- or X-rated, from the local video store.

Sex addicts learn to escape their feelings through compulsions or addictions. Many have several major addictions and a longer list of "minor" ones. Dr. Carnes has discovered in his research that the more severe the childhood abuse experience has been, the more likely it is that a sex addict will have multiple addictions.[2] This makes sense. The more painful the childhood experience has been the more escapes an addict will need to medicate the pain.

This means that in recovery sex addicts may have trouble with other addictions, and there may be significant emotional and spiritual issues left to work on. If sex is the primary way a person escapes the emotional and spiritual issues, stopping sex will only bring those issues to the surface. The person must first learn how to deal with those issues in a healthy way before he or she can deal with the addiction itself.

Sex addicts may wonder, "When will all these addictions stop?" It is discouraging to battle many addictive behaviors, but they may suffer from what has been called an "addictive personality."[3] People who are this addictive can turn to many behaviors or substances and become addicted to them quite easily if they are not careful.

THE SEXUAL ADDICTION CYCLE

The behaviors and characteristics of sexual addiction can be understood by what Dr. Carnes has described as the Sexual Addiction Cycle. (See figure 2.)

Sexual addicts, like all addicts, are ashamed and seek to escape this feeling through addictive activity; however, that behavior in turn increases the sense of shame. Escaping shame through addiction that in turn increases shame is one cycle that a sexual addict experiences. This cycle needs to be understood in order to recover from sexual addiction.

The first part of the sexual addiction cycle is *preoccupation*. Rather than allowing themselves to experience their shame, pain, and loneliness, sex addicts will start thinking about sex. Preoccupation involves the building-block behavior of sexual fantasy.

This preoccupation, in itself, produces pleasurable and exciting sensations, creating a positive mood in order to avoid a negative one. This can be used at any time of the day in any situation. Often sex addicts may seem like they are not present even if they physically are.

Preoccupation also creates a desire to act out the thoughts. Before acting out can occur, some planning is necessary. This phase of the sexual addiction cycle is called the *ritual*. Rituals are as varied in number as there are sex addicts. They may be very simple or very complex.

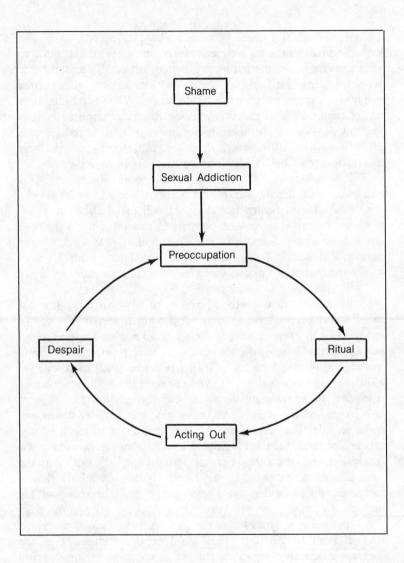

Figure 2: The Carnes's Sexual Addiction Cycle

An addict may come home at night, pick up the TV guide, look for provocative movies, and watch them. While at work an addict may go into the bathroom to masturbate. They might also get into their car, go to the bank for money, then cruise neighborhoods where they can purchase sex. When traveling, a sex addict might look in the phone book for telephone numbers of massage parlors and call them to get prices. Many sex addicts have lists of available partners and have only to call, stop by, or otherwise make the connection with these partners to become sexual.

Rituals may take five minutes or five hours. Some sex addicts will travel great distances to obtain pornography and won't act out with it until they return home. Some will make elaborate travel plans in order to connect with partners from around the country or around the world. Sometimes the ritual will involve accumulating nonsexual materials that are used in the sexual acting out. One sex addict always bought plastic sheets to cover his apartment so as not to "soil" it with his sexual activity.

Recruiting new partners creates rituals that may last for months and years. A man may meet a woman and at first simply engage her in conversation, telling her jokes that involve sexual humor. If she laughs, the conversation, over time, may regularly include this kind of "teasing." He invites her to lunch and they have a number of lunches together. The conversation begins to involve disclosing more intimate details of each other's lives.

At this point in the ritual the two people consider themselves to be friends. They enjoy their sharing but begin to feel a certain excitement and sexual longing. Perhaps even years after their original conversation they become sexual with each other. At the time when sex happens, it may seem to the sex addict that it happened all of a sudden and was "spontaneous." This is absurd. He or she has been soliciting this experience since the original meeting.

Just like the fantasies in the preoccupation stage, the ritual may in itself be exciting. This could be the excitement of the romance in discovering a new partner. It could be exciting to find some new form of pornography or a massage parlor that practices certain techniques that haven't been experienced before. Some sexual addiction cycles contain risk, like going to bars in dangerous neighborhoods or having "secret" meetings with potential partners. This danger and excitement produces adrenalin, which is itself addictive.

Once sex addicts have reached the ritual stage it is almost inevitable that they will go on to the next stage: *acting out*. I have already described various kinds of acting out. Acting out does not just happen like a sudden thunderstorm. There is always conscious and unconscious thought behind it—preoccupation, preparation, and the ritual. When Christians say to a sex addict, "Stop acting out," they must also be prepared to help them stop thinking and planning.

Sexual addiction seems unmanageable because acting out just seems to "happen." Sex addicts must learn that this is really not the case. One addict recently described to me going to a distant city. When he got there, he got in his rental car, headed for the instant teller machine, then drove to a massage parlor. "It was as if the car was on automatic pilot," he said. I asked him when he first knew he was going to this city. The answer was months before. Had he ever been there before? Yes. Had he ever been to that massage parlor before? Yes. When did he start thinking about the possibility of going there again? He had for several weeks before the trip. The reality is that he had been preoccupied about going to that massage parlor for weeks, made sure he had enough money in his instant teller account, and had his own car to get there! This acting out did not happen in several minutes; it took several weeks.

Once acting out has occurred, the final stage of the cycle occurs: *despair*. Sex addicts wanted to stop but once again didn't. They committed more shameful activity, and now they feel weak, perverted, and helpless. Anxious about being found out, they fall into a deep depression.

The stage of despair is a form of depression. Many sex addicts are deeply depressed whether or not they are aware of it. Those around them would certainly know that they have "black moods," and might even question them about their moodiness. Sex addicts have learned not to talk about their feelings so they would deny this if asked. They also have great tolerance for pain and would deny to themselves that they feel as badly as they do.

Depression at this level can lead to other problems that are symptoms of depression, including insomnia, overeating or not eating, inability to concentrate, hypersensitivity, and mood swings. Most symptoms of depression express themselves physically in headaches, backaches, fatigue, and stomach disorders. Susceptibility to infections and even cancer can also result from chronic depression. I would wager to say that a majority of visits to a doctor's office are the result of depression-related physical symptoms.

Ultimately, the stage of despair leads to thoughts of suicide. The shame and hopelessness is such that the only way out seems to be death. If sex addiction is in fact a disease, the ultimate consequence of any disease left untreated is death.

The despair may also be full of anger and blame. "It is God's fault, he didn't help me again." Or "It was their fault, they seduced me again." Or "If we could only get rid of the pimps, pornographers, and prostitutes, I would be all right." To a sex addict it may seem easier to control others, including culture itself, than to control one's self.

What are sex addicts to do about this despair? They do not know how to get help, and they are too ashamed to confess their activities to anyone who might help. To escape their despair, then, they return to the old cycle of preoccupation with sex, ritual, acting out, and despair. The downward spiral begins anew.

OBSERVABLE SYMPTOMS

While sexual addicts will attempt to conceal their behavior, they usually exhibit some readily observable symptoms. People who live, work, or worship with a sex addict might notice these symptoms.

As you read through these symptoms, be careful when you use them to judge the behavior of others. Some of these symptoms might indicate other addictions or emotional problems. If you see someone exhibiting these symptoms, that person may need help and probably doesn't have the strength or tools to be able to ask for it.

Here is a brief list of observable symptoms:

1. *Preoccupation with sexual behaviors.* Sex addicts will first of all be extremely preoccupied with their own sexual fantasies. This preoccupation leads them to search for sexual expression of their fantasies. They will devote more and more time to the preoccupation until they get to a point where sexual thoughts and activities are the *central organizing principle of their lives.*

How will someone else notice this? There are many ways. Is there pornography of any type around? Do they watch sexually explicit videos? Are there X- or R-rated videos lying around? Do they point out or notice sexually oriented places like bookstores, massage parlors, or striptease bars? Do they do "double takes" of attractive people? Does their conversation seem to center on sexual activity?

If you are this person's sexual partner, does he or she ask for sex incessantly, or never ask you? Does he or she complain about lack of sex or ask for sexual practices that you don't enjoy?

These are some of the more obvious indications. In a more subtle way, if you live around a sex addict, you will almost have a "feeling" of sexual energy. Even though you may not be factually aware of the sexual practices that are taking place, you will have an intuitive sense that something is wrong.

2. *Escalating patterns of sexual activity.* Sexual addiction is a degenerative disease, and the amount or level of activity will get worse. For example, it may seem normal to go to R-rated movies because lots of people do. In early stages, sex addicts may scan movie reviews to see which ones have sex actually portrayed in them. From that they graduate to R-rated movies from the video store. Next, they move on to X-rated videos, and from there they may frequent more dangerous places for hard-core pornography.

The patterns of escalation can be as varied as there are numbers of sex addicts. They may be short or long. They may vary in intensity. Remember that sex addicts can go for long periods of time without acting out. This may fool them or others into thinking that their disease is under control. More serious behaviors may alternate with less serious ones. In fact, sex addicts may commit less serious behaviors in order to stop greater ones, or *reward* themselves with lesser ones for not committing the more serious forms. In the final analysis, however, the acting out will always escalate.

3. *Acting distant or withdrawn.* As the pattern of sexual activity escalates, sex addicts will seem more distant and withdrawn because they are preoccupied with their sexual activity, guilt, shame, and the fear of getting caught. They will be unavailable mentally and often physically to everyone around them. They may seem distant or cold, or they may even become angry if they are badgered about what they are thinking. Ask them what the trouble is and they will deny any problems. More and more their work, activity, interests, and relationships will suffer from lack of attention.

4. *Depression and mood swings.* Sex addicts may be alternately depressed and then excited, even giddy. In the sexual addiction cycle, the withdrawn character of preoccupation is followed by the excitement of the ritual or the chase, the high of acting out, and then the despair or shame. To ask them about these mood changes would elicit elaborate denials and perhaps even rage.

5. *Irritability.* Sex addicts try to avoid their feelings and avoid being found out. They create enormous defenses. If anyone were to ask questions that would come too close to the truth or simply challenge their story, addicts can become greatly irritated. The behavior of sex addicts makes them angry at themselves and angry at others. Abuse issues of the past also create hidden resentments and angers. Triggers that remind them of these past events may set off anger that seems unrelated to the importance of the event. Simple questions, insignificant events, or basic statements may incite an angry reaction that will surprise you because the reaction is out of proportion to the event.

6. *Abuse of self or others.* If sex addicts have been abused in the past, they may do the same to others. If they have not been talked to, they won't talk to others. If they have been yelled and screamed at, they will yell and scream at others. If they have been preached to, they will preach to others. They will abuse others in ways they were

abused. Victims of this abuse may believe this is acceptable behavior, or they may be too afraid or ashamed to confront it.

Sex addicts may also abuse themselves. Their personal habits and hygiene, their eating, smoking, and drinking may annoy everyone around them. They may engage in any activity or use any substance compulsively. I met one sex addict who chewed three packs of gum while exercising for three hours every day.

Many sex addicts tell intimate details of their lives, except the sexual details, to strangers. A Catholic bishop told me about one priest who had almost every member of this church thinking he or she was the priest's personal confidant. When his sexual acting out was discovered, everyone was shocked by it and felt guilty that they hadn't known. Sex addicts are trying to get people to like them by seeming to confide in them. Sex addicts have lots of acquaintances, but no friends.

7. *Resistance to supervision or criticism.* Since they hide a large part of their daily behaviors, sex addicts are not very open to criticism, whether it is constructively given or not. They may live with people who would very much like to correct their behaviors and who continue to turn up the volume of their criticisms in order to be heard. This just drives sex addicts deeper into withdrawal, for they do not want their sexual behaviors to be challenged or threatened by supervision.

8. *Use of sexual humor.* Sex addicts may use sexual humor all the time. They are always teasing (which many consider sexual harassment) or telling sexual jokes. Sex addicts "sexualize" most situations and see some sexual humor in it. Sexual jokes can be used to recruit new sexual partners. Sex addicts can gauge the reaction of a person hearing their sexual joke, and if that reaction is favorable, the level of sexual engagement might be taken one step higher.

Sex addicts are great at double entendre—words or phrases that might have two meanings, one of them sexual. Say something in this fashion and the sex addict will smile and point out the sexual content. If a person says, "My friend was able to get off on time this morning," a sex addict will interpret *get off* to be about orgasm and will make some sexual joke about it.

9. *Inappropriate sexual behavior and overt sexual advances.* Know what to look for and you can spot a sex addict at a party, the grocery store, even at church. They tell sexual jokes, they touch people in ways that don't feel right, they give too many hugs, and they are *looking*, always looking. Their eyes dart here and there. They take everything in. They follow certain attractive people.

Some sex addicts are very direct. They will come right up to you and talk about sex. One day the receptionist at a health club told me a man had just come up to her, out of the blue, and asked if she would like to go home with him. There are more subtle overtures than this, and sex addicts can be very creative.

As the disease progresses, the kinds of inappropriate sexual behavior will get worse. A pastor's wife told me of how her husband first took her to R-, then X-rated movies. Next he bought a video camera and wanted to film her nude. Then he wanted to film her being sexual with other men. When she refused, he became angry and abusive. She left and he never has received help. The strange part about stories like this is how long it may take a loved one to challenge the behavior. Look for it in the early days. The progression of the disease means that the consequences will get worse.

Spouses should be aware that sex addicts will increasingly be frustrated with sexual activity in marriage. They may learn to avoid sex altogether as a result of frustration or as a result of sexual activity outside of marriage. Sex addicts may make increasing demands for sex and certain types of sexual activity, or they may not be interested in sex at all.

An uneducated spouse will feel guilty that he or she can't fulfill the marital "obligation," as well as feeling angry at or repulsed by the demands. It is difficult for Christian spouses to confront inappropriate sexual demands in marriage because they may assume it is their duty to be submissive. However, they need to assert their right to have sexual standards and preferences.

An educated spouse will know that no amount of sexual activity or level of attractiveness will be enough to satisfy an unrecovering sex addict. Even if the sex in marriage may seem quite good, he or she might not be aware of the partner's frustrations because the sex addict doesn't have the ability to articulate them.

10. *Occupational, social, family, professional, and legal difficulties.* As the disease progresses, increasing amounts of time will be spent thinking about and obtaining sex. This means there will be less time for work, social life, family, professional responsibilities, or any other obligations. Ignoring these activities is evidence that energy is being drained off somewhere else. A concerned person should demand to know what is going on. Family members have a right to know because they are the victims.

If work is ignored, there will be loss of jobs and income. Friendships or other social relationships will be lost. Unethical conduct can result in the loss of professional licenses or the ability to practice the profession. Finally, if illegal behavior is involved, a sex addict may be arrested and could go to jail. Many sex addicts try to explain away arrests, such as for soliciting prostitution, as isolated events that won't happen again. Don't be fooled! These arrests are rarely, if ever, isolated. More than likely they are part of a long-standing pattern.

It is important to look for obligations, duties, jobs, and relationships that are being ignored before there are great losses and consequences. There still might not be anything that can be done at these early stages to help sex addicts. Some of them need to bottom out.

11. *Intuition.* Most spouses, bosses, pastors, or friends of sex addicts have a sixth sense that something is wrong. This may take various forms and could simply be a combination of impressions from certain events. They may feel they are not getting the full or the real story. The explanations of sex addicts for where they were or what they were doing on such and such an occasion just don't make sense.

One spouse told me her husband used to take thirty to forty-five minutes to take the baby-sitter home. He would explain that he was just visiting or that he had stopped off at the convenience store and then just driven around to relax. He sounded convincing and sincere, but it didn't make sense. In fact, he was briefly visiting a woman with whom he was having an affair.

People with this kind of intuition must trust their instincts. My experience is that God gives us intuition, a built-in barometer of our comfort level. People must trust that barometer when it lets them know they are uncomfortable. It is not a caring reaction to look the other way and hope that things will get better, for the sex addict is slowly dying, and things will only get worse.

12. *Direct evidence.* Don't ignore the direct evidence: charge card bills from companies with strange names, phone bills with unfamiliar or 900-numbers, pornographic magazines, and so on. The spouse may be the last one to accept this evidence. A part of them doesn't want the pain of accepting the truth. The spouse may even become involved in elaborate explanations of why it can't be true. You have heard it said that "The family is often the last one to know." They aren't the last to know, but they may be the last to accept the facts.

If you suspect that someone is a sexual addict, there are definitely things that can be done. These are discussed in section three. Before going to that section, it is vitally important to know where sexual addiction comes from and what causes it in order to know how to help. But first we need to examine the unhappy phenomenon of sexually addicted pastors.

5

Sexually Addicted Pastors

As a twelve-year-old boy, Peter was sexually molested by a man in a public park. When he told his local priest in the confessional, the priest wanted to hear explicit details and eventually persuaded Peter to perform the same acts with him.

As a young man, Peter engaged in anonymous sexual activity with other men. He sought to stop this behavior, but his career led him to many places where sexual connections were easy. Eventually he decided to enter the priesthood, thinking that he could alleviate his sense of shame by joining himself to God and that people would respect him if he were a "father" to them. He also hoped his vow of celibacy would keep him from further acting out.

This was not to be the case. In seminary, his homosexual acting out continued with classmates and progressively became more active. Later, as a parish priest, he began to seduce altar boys and boys from the youth group who were the same age he was when first molested. Finally, Peter was arrested. Fortunately for him, he was able to get treatment for sexual addiction.

A WIDESPREAD PROBLEM

The problem of pastoral sexual misconduct is a large one. A *Leadership* magazine survey revealed that twenty-three percent of the three hundred pastors who responded had done something sexually inappropriate with someone other than their spouse.[1] Twelve percent of the pastors have engaged in intercourse with people other than their spouse. Tim LaHaye noticed that, at one point, the churches of the city of Dallas all seemed under attack because so many pulpits were vacated by sexual disgrace.[2] Nationally known evangelists such as Jim Bakker and Jimmy Swaggart have brought large-scale media attention to this problem.

Our legal system is also forcing the church to look seriously at pastoral sexual misconduct. Civil lawsuits are being filed by hundreds of victims against pastors for the emotional damage created by sexual abuse and exploitation. Some victims have even sued whole denominations for keeping situations quiet and for transferring clergy. As one Catholic bishop told me, "It used to be that when a priest committed sexual misconduct, we kept it as quiet as possible. We tried to control the damage, and we transferred the priest. We can no longer get away with that."

UNHEALED WOUNDERS

Christians have great difficulty dealing with the sexual sins of their leaders. It is essential, therefore, that we understand the characteristics of sexually addicted clergy. Healing of the church and its members can only begin when pastors are able to deal with their secret sin and heal their own wounds. As leaders, they possess the spiritual authority to model healing.

Pastors tend to be placed on pedestals and are expected to be perfectly spiritual. They are a symbol to others that it is possible to have faith. When they commit sin it is very threatening. Observers might wonder, "If a minister falls, what will happen to me?"

In his book *The Wounded Healer*, pastoral psychologist Henri Nouwen characterizes pastors as caring people who are often wounded by the sins, hurts, and burdens of their people; by their workload; and by loneliness. If they take care of themselves by getting help and support when they need it, they can grow stronger and wiser and become more compassionate and effective healers. Thus they become "wounded healers": true shepherds of both themselves and others.

But some ministers don't know how to care for their own wounds. They remain lonely, resentful, burned out, and angry. When they are not healed themselves they are likely to injure others as they search for nurturing, for ways to express their anger, and for ways to escape their feelings. Father Gil Gustafson, a priest of the Archdiocese of Minneapolis and St. Paul, calls these pastors "unhealed wounders."

THE PASTOR'S RESPONSIBILITY

Historically, the church has kept very quiet about pastors who commit sexual immorality. A minister may have been "defrocked," depending on the denomination, but more than likely he simply "left." Perhaps the pastor was transferred or found a new call. We tend to hope that the "geographic cure" will take effect, repentance will take place, and sexual sinning will stop. This seldom happens. Many pastors leave a trail of sexual misconduct in many locations.

The church may also assume that when a pastor has an affair, it is not the pastor's fault. Perhaps the pastor was under too much stress. Or perhaps the pastoral spouse is to blame for not taking care of the pastor's needs. Or the devil is to blame—maybe the devil pursues and tempts pastors more.

We must begin by understanding that, whatever the circumstances, pastoral sexual misconduct is ultimately the pastor's responsibility. Even if a person has pursued the pastor and tried to seduce him, it is still the pastor's responsibility to refuse, just as Joseph refused Potiphar's wife.

Although it is a pastor's duty to keep himself or herself from sexual sin, there are many factors that contribute to the high incidence of sexual sin in the pastorate. Here we will look at the combination of factors that contribute to pastoral sexual immorality.

THE CONGREGATION

Church members tend to look to pastors with respect and devotion. We give them spiritual authority. We trust them. In many ways we look on them as we would a parent: we seek their pastoral love and approval and want to benefit from their spirituality.

Some church members are simply attracted to the pastor. He or she is powerful and charismatic, gentle and understanding. Whether a pastor is physically attractive or not, there can be a sexual energy to this attraction.

Church members who have been sexually abused as children have learned to get approval from their parents through being sexual. If these people view their pastor as a parent and need his approval, they might also think they will need to be sexual with him. When sex takes place between this kind of person and the pastor, it is essentially incest, a parental figure being sexual with a childlike figure. Although it seems to be sex between two consenting adults, it is actually exploitative sex. Both sexual exploitation (sex between adults in which one adult uses the other) and sexual abuse (sex between an adult and a child) are punishable. In fact, there are pastors serving jail terms for sexually exploiting their parishioners.

BEING ORDAINED TO REDUCE SHAME

The position of authority that a pastor is given can appeal to persons with low self-esteem. They may (perhaps unconsciously) think, "I am a worthless person, but if I become a pastor, people will like me, trust me, and think I'm worth something." A sex addict who is full of shame and wants to control his or her behaviors might also think, "If I become a pastor, my special relationship to God will change me, take away my lust, and prevent me from sexual immorality."

Ruth entered the pastorate to escape the shame of her past. Molested and physically abused by a brother and her father, she found sanctuary in her church youth group. At age eighteen she escaped her family to go to college. There she participated in the activities of a campus church and at one point became sexually involved with the campus pastor.

Then Ruth began to pursue physically abusive relationships

with men that she dated. In some ways she was encouraging this, even enjoying it, because violent sex had been "normal" to her as a child. However, her behavior also caused her deep shame.

Recognizing that her "escape" early in life had been through the church, Ruth decided that more church involvement might give her a more permanent escape. She entered seminary and was eventually ordained. Then, during a seminary internship, she discovered bars that helped people make connections for the purpose of physically abusive sexual activity, and she allowed herself to be tied and beaten up on a regular basis. After she became a parish pastor she drove into the city on her day off, her clerical garb providing good "cover" for the bruises she received.

After a while, Ruth began to wonder why her ordination hadn't "taken." She began to investigate ordination in another denomination. Finally, a therapist convinced her to be treated for sexual addiction. There she realized that in her ordination she had expected to be transformed. She thought her entire being would be different, that she would no longer desire to be physically beaten and that lust would be taken away. She had been ordained to reduce her shame, but it didn't work.

CODEPENDENCY AND ENABLING

Codependency is an addiction to approval. The codependent person will do almost anything to gain approval.

Sexual addicts are usually codependent. They need a great deal of approval from others because they can't give it to themselves. Sexually addicted pastors might think, "What better place to gain approval from lots of people than in a congregation?"

Once after I gave a lecture on codependency, a retired pastor's wife came to me and said, "What you are calling codependency is what in seminary we were taught was helping others." This woman thought I was advocating selfishness as a healthier posture.

However, I was not encouraging selfishness so much as discouraging codependent and enabling behavior. *Enabling* is a word that is also used quite frequently in the addiction community to describe those who "enable" a person to continue their addiction unchallenged. An enabler will take care of people to gain or maintain their approval.

In the pastoral role there is plenty of justification for "caretaking," for it is part of the job description. Addicted, co-dependent pastors take care of lots of people, thinking they will be liked and respected. Under the surface they may get angry at all they are expected to do, blaming the church for "too many demands." But they can't say no. If they did, someone might not like them.

Sexually addicted pastors might see aspects of their own woundedness in the person they seek to help. Certain members of their congregations might have similar abusive histories to those of their pastors. Pastors who experience this similarity may overidentify with these members. Caring for these members can be a vicarious way of trying to care for themselves.

DENIAL

The problem of denial is especially acute for sexually addicted pastors. For one thing, the consequences of sexual immorality are profound. This creates great fear, and denial can result. What's more, pastors are not supposed to have problems. Church people don't like their pastors to have problems. A sexually addicted pastor might say, "My role says that I need to be perfect. I take care of others. They look to me. People need me to be their spiritual leader, their inspiration. I can't admit to any problems, much less sexual ones."

Rather than ask for help, many pastors will go on leading their double life. This is intensely lonely. While they might be taking great care of their congregations, they are not taking care of themselves. They are dying spiritually.

A factor that makes it easy for pastors to deny their problems is that their daily activities are largely unsupervised. Their time is usually their own. They are not accountable to anyone. This free, unsupervised time is deadly.

Add to this the fact that pastors are so looked up to that most people in the congregation will be afraid to confront them. A church member might ask, "Who am I to challenge our pastor's behaviors?"

WITHDRAWAL

Another universal feature of sexual addiction is withdrawal, the act of distancing oneself from others. The role of pastor offers built-in excuses to withdraw. Pastors are supposed to contemplate and meditate. They are expected to have many deep concerns on their mind.

Sexually addicted pastors can escape by working in their study. As the addiction progresses they will seem more and more withdrawn. In the height of the disease a normally social pastor may cut off most contact with the outside world. Besides denying their problem, withdrawn sexually addicted pastors will also avoid supervision by mentors, superiors, or other professionals.

It is easy for pastors to say, "I have a meeting downtown, or a hospital call to make, or a sermon to write. I need some time alone in my study. I'm in prayer. Don't bother me." Who would bother such a spiritual person on such spiritual business? It will always shock us later on to find out that this spiritual business might really have been sexual in nature. If a pastor seems unable to account for his time, he might be withdrawing. It is the responsibility of the congregation, or its leadership, to require accountability.

Is it intrusive to ask pastors to document their activities? I don't think so. While on the surface they may be angry and defensive, underneath they are ashamed of their double life. A part of them will be grateful to be confronted.

BLACKOUTS

Addicts of all kinds experience blackouts. Sexually addicted pastors may not be able to remember periods of time. Perhaps they will claim to be preoccupied with important matters, even naming it a "spiritual preoccupation." They might also claim to be busy, running from place to place. They might miss appointments or forget important events. If this happens more and more, these are signs that the disease is progressing.

RIGIDITY

Sexually addicted pastors seek in many ways to control their disease. They may teach rigid formulas, or follow certain routines. They may think that if they win enough church members, if the budget is large enough, if they make enough calls, or if they counsel enough, then they will be rewarded with relief from sexual temptations.

This kind of thinking reflects a cycle of guilt in which a pastor tries to expiate sexual sins by doing good works. When more sexual sins take place, more good works need to follow. This cycle of guilt is also a cycle of burnout.

BLAMING

Rigidity and denial lead to blaming. Addicts don't take responsibility for themselves and look to the behavior of others to explain why they do what they do. Sexually addicted pastors can point the finger at others and add theological justification for their behavior. They may argue, "How could it be my fault that I sexually acted out? There is so much sexual temptation out there in the world."

The sexually addicted pastor who has exploited a parishioner may use what I call the "Potiphar's Wife Defense." Those who attend seminary are warned about potentially seductive females. But seldom is there instruction in pastors' responsibilities or the weaknesses of people under the influence of pastoral power. When a pastor has sex with a parishioner, it has been easy to blame the parishioner.

REACTION FORMATION

Rigidity, blaming, and denial will also lead to what we call "reaction formation." This behavior involves reacting to phenomena in others that you are concerned about in yourself. A sexually addicted pastor will react to sexual sins "out there" in others and in the world. This reaction reflects the need to control the sexual temptation in others in order to control oneself. Jimmy Swaggart ranted and railed against "prostitutes, pimps, and pornographers" while at the same time being involved with prostitutes. This is reaction formation. Ironically, the hypocrisy of his preaching and his attempts to reveal the sexual sins of other pastors led one pastor to hire a private detective to expose him.

LOSS OF PERSONAL VALUES

Sexual addicts, particularly as their disease progresses, experience a loss of personal values. When they hear of a sexual sin, people often ask, "How could they do such a thing; don't they know any better?" Sexually addicted pastors generally *do* know better. They are aware of rules, laws, restrictions, and morals. But their addiction is so unmanageable that they pursue it anyway. They will also tell themselves that it is all right to break some of the rules, some of the time. They may argue that they aren't hurting their family or congregation by being involved in masturbation or pornography. Even when caught abusing or exploiting a parishioner they will have elaborate justifications about how the sexual activity is part of caring pastoral activity.

We will see in chapter 6 that many sexual addicts are abuse victims. Like Ruth, they have learned to accept abusive experiences as "normal."

SEX EQUALS LOVE

The only physical nurturing some sex addicts received as children was sexual in nature. Never having experienced healthy touching of any kind, they search desperately for nurturing and begin to equate it with sex.

Pastors may delude themselves into thinking that since they are caregivers, anything they do—including sexual activity—will be caring. Many pastors who are sexual exploiters and abusers have said to me that their victims needed love, understanding, and care. It seemed natural to nurture them, but this nurturing often led to sex.

A pastor might be counseling with a woman who has a bad marriage. As she tells the details of her lonely life the pastor really does begin to care for her. He may then say to himself, "I will be the first understanding man in her life. I will show her what healthy sex with a 'gentle' man is like." Under this "caring delusion," some pastors *really* do think that sex equals love and is a caring activity.

THE MYTH OF THE PERFECT PERSON

The selfishness of sexual exploitation can be an extension of sexual addicts' belief that there is a perfect person out there to nurture them. For many, sexual addiction is the pursuit of this perfect partner. Having been abandoned by one or more significant persons in their life, they seek a perfect person to fill their loneliness.[3] If they are married, they will have given up on the idea that their spouse is this person, and anger and frustration result.

A typical congregation is full of such persons. They may perceive the all-wise, all-caring pastor to be such a savior. If they seek to fulfill needs that their parents left unfilled, they will project on the pastor qualities of their parents, hoping that the pastor will be a better parent.

The sexually addicted pastor and the needy parishioner are mutual elements in a very explosive situation. The parishioner will do anything for the pastor, even violate moral boundaries. They may imagine themselves to be the person who will take care of the pastor in ways that others, including the pastoral spouse, don't. They may also get a sense of power from being involved with this "saint." Ultimately, of course, the responsibility for sexual activity rests with the pastor.

ANGER

Addicts experience much anger, sometimes unconsciously and sometimes consciously. Usually they don't have the tools to express this in healthy ways. It is then repressed and becomes a deep and long-lasting depression, or it may be expressed in indirect and passive ways.

Sexually addicted pastors may allow themselves to feel abused by their role, feeling their congregations are taking advantage of them. The sex addict's core belief is that "no one takes care of me but myself." This attitude fuels the sexually addicted pastors' inclination to take advantage of people who offer them sex.

Sexually addicted pastors may also experience gender hatred. If a pastor is angry at all women, it may be that all women remind him of his abusive mother. Whatever woman is in his office at any particular moment will be in danger of that anger.

It is widely believed that people who abuse and exploit sexually are angry at their victims. It is certainly true that anger, so early developed, can be a part of any act of sexual abuse or exploitation. In helping pastors who commit these sins, we must recognize that their anger at men or women is often the symptom of much deeper, unhealed anger at others who have hurt them.

ENTITLEMENT

One reason sexual addicts feel they can express anger in any way is that they believe they deserve to get their needs met. The sense of entitlement is particularly dangerous for sexually addicted pastors. Their role places them in great isolation and at the same time makes many demands on them. As they seek to fulfill these demands they may also come to believe that they deserve to get some rewards. They are lonely and don't know how to reach out to others in healthy ways to meet their needs except through sexual addiction. Perhaps anger allows them to cross definite boundaries. Or perhaps it is their depression, loneliness, or desperation to get some nurturing.

The wife of an evangelist told me about her husband's numerous sexual encounters with women who came to him for counseling after a revival. "I just did a good job, I won a lot of souls for Christ, now I need to take care of myself," he would tell himself. "These women seem so grateful and willing. I am a loving person. They won't be harmed by this, and I am entitled to it."

THE DELUSION OF SPECIAL PROTECTION

Sexual addicts are guilty of magical thinking. "If I am good, good will come to me. If I am bad, bad will come to me." Sexually addicted pastors guilty of "bad things" will try to cover their sins with more "good things." They continually try to keep a positive balance with God so that they won't be punished.

Sexually addicted clergy also have a hope that their ordination makes them special and perhaps protected by God. This delusion may cause them to take great risks that may bring danger to the clergy or to others. Risk also brings with it excitement, a high that in itself can be addicting.

In cases of sexual abuse or exploitation, the delusion of sexually addicted pastors is that they won't get caught, that they are specially protected, and that what they are doing is all right because they are ordained. This delusion is very dangerous. It allows sexually addicted clergy to *believe* that their activity is, in fact, not damaging to their victims. They may even delude themselves into believing the opposite of the truth: "If I denied myself to them they would feel abandoned."

Yet sexual addicts also, paradoxically, *want* to be caught. Their disease is unmanageable, and they know they can't stop on their own. Unconsciously, they may slip up and do things that reveal their secret. When they are found out, they may be afraid and ashamed, but they will also be relieved.

WARNING SIGNS

There are several warning signs that might prompt a congregation or its leadership to ask more questions concerning its clergy.

1. *Symptoms of depression.* The pastor is normally positive or content but now seems depressed or moody.
2. *Mood swings.* The pastor's moods seem to fluctuate wildly. Sometimes the pastor does lots of work, at other times no work gets done.
3. *Lots of alone time.* The pastor always seems to be alone and doesn't like questions regarding this.
4. *Counseling at strange times and places.* The pastor is seen counseling people late at night, behind closed doors, in restaurants, or in frequent home visits to one particular church member.
5. *Trouble in the pastor's marriage.* The spouse seems depressed or angry. Rumors float around about the unhappiness of the marriage.
6. *Pastor uses sexual humor.* This could be a form of sexual exhibitionism and, depending on people's reactions, a form of sexual recruitment.
7. *Pastor seems to touch people often.* Some parishioners are uncomfortable with the touches or hugs.
8. *Pastor seems lonely.* He or she may tell lots of people about this in superficial ways, not really asking for help, just complaining about needs that are never met.
9. *Pastor preaches about his or her own personal issues.* People will come out of church feeling sorry for the poor pastor, but no one knows how to help because there hasn't been a direct request.
10. *Pastor is seen frequenting places where pornography or sexual activity is known to be available.*
11. *Rumors abound regarding the pastor's sexual activities.*

This is a partial list. Many of these symptoms could point to other kinds of personal trouble besides sexual addiction. However, when you see these warning signs, the responsible thing to do is to ask the pastor what is going on.

When Nathan confronted King David about his adultery, David was publicly humiliated. However, he accepted his sin, confessed it, asked for forgiveness, and accepted the consequences. These signs of David's acceptance of his sinfulness were also signs of his potential for health. I believe that Nathan confronted David not to judge him but to restore him to relationship with God.

There are thousands of sexually addicted clergy who are alone, discouraged, and afraid. Who can they talk to about their problems, their woundedness? If we are not to shoot our wounded, we must understand the problems involved. And we must follow the example of Nathan the Prophet in resolving the problems.

Sexually addicted pastors *can* be healed. However, as they themselves know, they have a lifetime disease. If they have exploited or abused parishioners, they should not be restored to their position, not only to protect the victims, but also to protect the addict from falling back into the addictive behavior.

I have known many sexually addicted clergy who have found healing. Humble and penitent about the damage they have done to themselves and others, they are in many ways healthier than some of their colleagues. They have learned from their pain and are stronger and wiser. They have gone from being unhealed wounders to being wounded healers. Is there not some place for them in the church? After all, King David was allowed to keep Bathsheba as his wife, and he remained king for another thirty years.

Finally, to those pastors who recognize some of their own behaviors, be of good courage. Despite your worst behaviors there is still the promise of grace. You can stop hurting yourself and others, but only if you reach out for help. May you find the strength to ask for that help now.

Part II

Roots of Sexual Addiction—The Secret Sin of the Family

6.

Unhealthy Families

Sexual addiction begins in unhealthy families. Take the case of Roger. Roger's mother fondled his genitals when he was between the ages of one to three years old. Later one of his uncles made him perform oral sex. An aunt had intercourse with Roger when he was a teenager. Roger had an ongoing sexual relationship with a sister one year younger than himself until they both left home.

On the surface, however, Roger's family seemed a model family. Roger's dad was a busy, successful businessman who was involved in numerous civic activities. The whole family was very active in their local church. Roger, the oldest son, was expected to enter his father's business. In high school he started doing various jobs around the factory. His father, normally rather passive at home, yelled and screamed when Roger didn't get something quite right.

Roger was a star athlete and good student in high school. Instead of going to college, he entered his father's business, where he fought continually with his father and two younger brothers. Roger married a woman with two daughters.

Roger began going to Alcoholics Anonymous for a drug and alcohol problem he had had since adolescence. He achieved sobriety, yet he still masturbates daily, goes to X-rated bookstores, frequents prostitutes, and has had a string of affairs. His wife found out about one of these and demanded that he change. His pastor encouraged him to be gentle with himself, to accept God's forgiveness, and to work on his marriage so as to remain faithful.

In Roger's "perfect family," sex was never talked about, nor were problems of any kind. Everyone was expected to perform in ways that were acceptable and admirable to the outside community. While Roger's family seemed wonderful to everyone else, the family members were distant and cold. Roger remembers masturbating alone in his room at the age of five. His mother had demonstrated to him at an early age how pleasurable this sensation felt, and he soon learned to use it to escape the loneliness and chaos of his family.

UNDERSTANDING THE ABUSIVE FAMILY

Roger's story is not unique. Like most sex addicts, Roger grew up in an unhealthy family. While his family was normal to the outside world, they were strangers, even enemies, to each other. Roger cannot recover from his sexual addiction until he understands the nature of the pain he felt growing up in this family.

Saying that a family is unhealthy, like Roger's, is not a moral judgment against that family. Many parents of unhealthy families are doing the best they can. Many families make unhealthy mistakes out of loving intentions. However, if parents have not learned how to give love in healthy ways, and if family members have not attained some degree of personal health and maturity, it is highly likely that the whole family will be unhealthy.

Some therapists estimate that as many as ninety-five percent of all families are unhealthy at least to some degree. That may sound harsh. When a family is unhealthy, however, family members will be deeply wounded. These wounds may be emotional, physical, sexual, or spiritual.

Sexual addicts attempt to escape family wounds and associated painful feelings by creating pleasurable feelings through sexual activity. It is important for sexual addicts to recognize that their sexual activity is an attempt to medicate old wounds and to find love. To begin, they must understand what their wounds are. Understanding wounds will lead sex addicts back to the dynamics involved in their families. Understanding unhealthy families will begin the process of healing.

Sexual addicts who are in recovery from their disease do not blame family members for their addiction. They also do not seek to avoid their own responsibility for getting well. Recovering addicts, however, must understand what wounds happened to them, that they didn't deserve them, that they may not have received the love and nurturing that they needed, and that many of the messages that they learned may have been wrong. Understanding these things is crucial to changing opinions of themselves and others. It is also crucial in finding the love and nurturing that they never got but always needed.

When addicts learn about their unhealthy families they may become angry, and they will need to grieve. It may take a number of years to work through this process, for powerful emotions will be stirred up.

Jesus told Nicodemus that in order to inherit the kingdom of God we must be born again (John 3:3). We must become like a child seeking God's nurturing care. For abuse victims, this thought can be extremely painful. However, becoming a child again can be healing if we understand and embrace the pain and begin to work through it. Jesus beckons the little children to come to him (Matt. 19:14), and he calls us his brothers and sisters. While our earthly family is imperfect, our heavenly Father is perfect. Knowing God the Father can allow us the freedom to accept our memories, to be born again, and to take comfort in him.

This chapter and the next one may stir up some painful memories for you. Don't run from them. Talk to someone who will listen and accept you. If necessary, get counseling from someone who knows how to work with these feelings.

In his ministry on earth, Jesus cast out demons which had "possessed" their victims and controlled their lives. Painful childhood memories are often like those demons. They are buried inside, and often people don't remember they are there. These unconscious memories of past events will cause people to react in certain ways to current situations. The next two chapters name some of these

BOUNDARIES	RULES	ROLES	ADDICTIONS
• Loose	• Don't talk	• Hero	• Substance
• Rigid	• Don't feel	• Scapegoat	Alcohol
	• Blame others	• Mascot	Drugs
	• Minimize	• Lost child	illegal
	• Deny	• Doer	prescription
		• Enabler	over the counter
		• Little prince/princess	Nicotine
		• Saint	Caffeine
			Food
			• Behavioral
			Sex
			Work
			Gambling
			Spending
			Shopping
			Eating
			Stealing
			Cleaning

Figure 3: Unhealthy Families

demons from the past in order to help the sex addict get well. When sex addicts know their demons, they can make healthy choices about getting rid of them.

What makes a family unhealthy? There are four categories of family dynamics that are helpful in answering this question: boundaries, rules, roles, and addictions. (See figure 3.)

BOUNDARIES

All families have boundaries. Boundaries are invisible areas of emotional, physical, sexual, and spiritual territory that exist around a person's body, mind, and soul. They are like a force field. They are your "space." Boundaries define the ways that a person's invisible space can and can't be crossed. When boundaries are maintained in a healthy way a person feels safe and protected. This is a nurturing environment.

In unhealthy families boundaries can become too *loose*. Interactions that shouldn't happen take place between family members. Boundaries are violated.

One evening I accidentally walked into my teenaged daughter's room while she was getting undressed. Although I quickly left, she was embarrassed, for I had stepped across an invisible boundary line. According to an unspoken boundary that says teenagers need privacy, I should have knocked before entering her room.

Boundary violations are more serious in an unhealthy family. Members of unhealthy families are hit, yelled at, sexually touched, or preached at inappropriately. When boundaries are too loose people learn that they don't have control over their bodies, minds, or spirits. Others invade their privacy. Someone older, someone bigger, someone they trusted does things to them and they can't stop it. Even saying "no" does no good. They find that the only way to please the other person is to cooperate, to open their boundaries, and to let the other person abuse them. These experiences affect how people relate to others, especially to loved ones and family, for the rest of their life.

Boundaries can also become too "rigid." Healthy interactions that should occur, don't. Loving and caring, listening and nurturing, guiding and witnessing, teaching and modeling, are not taking place. Children in these families feel as if they are held at arm's length. Starved for affection and attention, they begin to wonder, "What's wrong with me? I must be a bad person. Mom and Dad don't love me." To whom can these lonely children talk? They have learned that no one will listen. They feel abandoned. Later in life, they will seek to fill their loneliness with inappropriate and sinful behaviors.

Both loose and rigid boundaries can exist in the same family. One parent may cross a loose boundary while another is observing a rigid boundary. The child will experience both simultaneously. At different times different family members can be involved in this mixture of loose and rigid boundaries. The same person who commits incest can at other times be totally unloving. He or she violates boundaries that should be in place and erects other boundaries that should not exist.

When families demonstrate both loose and rigid boundaries, children are confused. The models they see are inconsistent and unpredictable. Later in life, if this child (now an adult) breaks some rule, someone may ask, "Didn't you know any better?" He or she may have known better intellectually, but was confused emotionally.

A prosecuting attorney asked a pastor, "Do you know which commandment says not to commit adultery?" The pastor did. The attorney then asked, "If you knew, why did you violate it?" The pastor knew right from wrong in his mind, but he had grown up with incest and other forms of sexual sin. In his experience, so many sexual boundaries had been crossed that he was emotionally confused about right and wrong.

Boundary confusion can be taught in more subtle ways than incest. I took my eight-year-old son to an air show where the ticket price for children seven and under was only two dollars. I was tempted to tell the ticket taker that he was seven, but if I had done so, I would have been teaching my son that in our family we can break rules.

Healthy families work to guard and nurture boundaries.

Growing up in this kind of family will create a feeling of being safe and loved.

RULES

A healthy family learns how to accept and talk about pain and feelings of loneliness, fear, anxiety, and anger. Unhealthy families feel that to talk about these emotions would make them worse. Members might say, "If I talk about my anger, it will get out of control—I might kill someone."

Unhealthy families have rules of conduct to prevent tension from getting out of control. These rules are probably never spoken or written down, but the whole family knows them and acts accordingly. Here are five of the most common:

1. *We don't talk.* Families may talk about superficial matters like the weather, sports, or some TV show, but they certainly don't talk about feelings, problems, or embarrassing situations. If members try to talk, they are ignored, teased, belittled, or simply told to be quiet. They might be told, "Big boys don't cry," or "Your brother never had a problem with that." Solutions are readily given to avoid talking: "I know your dog died. I'll get you a new one. It will be all right." Religion may be brought into it: "God doesn't like it when you are so sad." The rule may be proudly and simply verbalized, "In *this* family we don't talk about *that*" (whatever "that" may be).

2. *We don't feel.* This rule is specific to emotions. The feelings of family members are discouraged, particularly "negative" ones like anger, sadness, fear, or anxiety. The intent behind this rule is to be caring, but it becomes a form of denial. When a negative feeling begins to surface, the guardian of the "we don't feel" rule might say, "Please don't feel that way. Let me help you solve your problems." This is unhealthy because when people are talked out of their feelings, the feelings don't go away. They stay buried inside the person as long as they remain unexpressed. Buried feelings may be unconscious, but they can affect behavior for many years.

3. *We blame others for our problems.* Unhealthy families do not accept responsibility for their own problems or mistakes. To do so would create guilt over making a mistake and fear that someone will be mad at them or that something bad will happen. These families search for a scapegoat. A member might say, "You make me feel so angry." A healthy family member might say, "When you did that, I got angry. My anger belongs to me. I'd like to talk about what it was all about." Said in this way, the other person doesn't have to be defensive.

Direct statements of blame are heard every day in the school yard: "He hit me first, I had to hit him back," or "He called me a name, I had to hit him." Individuals, groups, and institutions are often the object of this blame. I remember getting off the hook for poor performance in the fourth grade by blaming my teacher for being inept, old, senile, and a Catholic who had it in for preachers' kids like me!

4. *We minimize our problems.* "That wasn't so bad" or "That was no big deal" is what we say when we are trying to convince others and ourselves that we aren't hurting or that we haven't hurt someone else. In unhealthy families this is based also on the perceived value of being of good courage, of not being a complainer, or of being a mature person. It can also be based on the belief that we are good people and that we don't cause harm to others. We create elaborate explanations as to why things are really better than they seem, for example, "Think of all those people in India who don't have any food to eat or clothes to wear. We should be thankful for what we do have."

Healthy families accept problems. They don't blow them out of proportion. They don't minimize problems. Rather, they place them in proper perspective and search for appropriate solutions while at the same time accepting the painful feelings the problems may create. A healthy family member might say, "That must really hurt. I'd like to hear about that. I'd also like to talk with you about ways we might try to prevent it from happening in the future."

5. *We deny our problems.* Unhealthy families deny that they have difficulties or have caused harm to themselves or to someone else. Family members might simply say, "I didn't mean to" or "I'm sorry. You'll forgive me won't you?" or "Why are you so upset? That was no big deal." These statements translate, "Don't blame me. It's not my fault. Don't be angry with me. Get off my back!" We think that if we deny our problems, we won't have to feel the pain of them.

Denial often takes the form of elaborate deceptions: lying, covering up, or looking the other way. For example, "That wasn't my car you saw at the motel" or "I was at the office working late on the books; it's almost tax time you know" or "I really don't know what you're talking about. I wasn't there."

The health of a family is a relative matter. There may be times when not talking about something is appropriate in order not to hurt or embarrass someone or break an important secret. Sometimes trying not to feel so bad or temporarily minimizing a problem are positive strategies which might allow us to get through a difficult time. Feelings can be talked about later when there is more time or it is safer to do so. There are times when someone really has done something wrong and deserves to be blamed or at least held accountable for the actions. This can be done in love and not in judgment. But there are also times when someone did nothing wrong and needs to deny it to an angry accuser.

ROLES

Roles are like parts in a play, defining the "job description" of each family member. Roles provide clear expectations of how to act in all family situations. They are given to a family member in spoken and unspoken ways. Roles will be unhealthy when they are inflexible and when they prevent someone from becoming the person God intends for them to be.

Roles are assigned at birth. The first child may be assigned to fulfill certain long-awaited expectations. Names may even illustrate what the family might hope for the child: "My grandfather John was a great man and a great lawyer; let's name our first son John." Maybe this new John doesn't want to be a great man or a great lawyer, but this may be the role he has been assigned.

The oral traditions of the family will be small and continual reminders of role expectations. Our new John may hear about his great grandfather, his wonderful exploits, his noble character, and his powerful legal adventures. The virtues of a law career will be extolled. On family vacations every law school passed will be pointed out. Later in life when John wonders about all of this, his parents might say, "We never *told* you to be a lawyer." Maybe they didn't directly. But young John was programmed to be one.

Roles are also based on what the family needs the child to be to maintain family functions. Some roles are culturally defined, such as the expectations that are automatically placed on boys or girls. Many authors have written about the system of the family and its roles. I have distilled those into eight roles:[1]

1. *The Hero.* Family heroes are expected to always excel. They will be the scholar, the athlete, or the social star. They will always be right, and the family will turn to them for answers. As heroes play their roles they will assume authority and be given special status. More time, attention, and money is devoted to their lessons, education, and activities. The rest of the family may be secretly jealous but will never talk about these feelings. Instead, everyone in the family can point to the hero and say, "See, we have this special person. We are a special family."

Elaborate historical stories will be created around heroes. Accounts of the achievements, victories, accomplishments, and any successes will be told at holiday times and other family gatherings. Pictures will be passed around, medals displayed, diplomas hung with care, and newspaper clippings neatly saved.

2. *The Scapegoat.* Scapegoats are the opposite of heroes. Scapegoats are expected to make mistakes, to be wrong, and to get into perpetual trouble. Their mistakes don't have to be major—just enough to attract attention to their stupidity or ineptness. Scapegoats are not expected to have talents or abilities, and they learn to hide gifts they do possess.

The unhealthy family feels it needs a scapegoat on whom to blame their problems. Somehow, consciously or unconsciously, the scapegoat learns this. What may later seem to be intentional or accidental mistakes could, in fact, be the result of learned patterns of reaction. Ultimately the family may ostracize the scapegoat or he or she may even choose to leave, thus earning the label of "black sheep of the family."

3. *The Mascot.* Mascots are the family comedians. Mascots may tell a joke, say something sarcastic, make fun of themselves or someone else, or get into mischief to get people to laugh. This behavior deflects attention away from feelings and does, in fact, relieve tension. For example, any sexual feelings or tension in the family will be dispelled with a sexual joke.

Humor in itself is not bad. Healthy families frequently laugh with each other. At appropriate times humor relieves tension and can bring healing. Because an unhealthy family does not like to express feelings, mascots use humor to avoid them. They get people to smile or laugh, but they bury their feelings. The feelings don't go away but wait beneath the surface to explode perhaps days, weeks, months, and even years later.

4. *The Lost Child.* The "lost child" learns that the family doesn't express feelings and particularly that his or hers will not be heard. So somewhere inside of themselves, lost children learned to bury their feelings. They go to their room and read books or play quietly. They may have imaginary friends and talk to them perhaps in a language that only they understand. To the outside world and to the family they may be the "quiet" or "serious" child, but they are more than this. Lost children are lost to themselves and to others, possessing deep feelings that they learn how to numb because no one will listen. Because there is no one to talk to, they gradually don't even recognize that they have feelings.

Later in life they may seem like strong silent types. They may even be admired for their ability to maintain their composure. They are "strong"; they can handle anything. If people ask them how they are, they quickly respond that they're fine. The lost child is set up to develop addictions of all kinds. They discover that an addictive substance or activity helps them to numb their feelings. Lost children are lonely, sad, and sometimes depressed.

5. *The Doer.* The doer is the family member who gets things done. Doers keep the family functioning by cooking the meals, paying the bills, doing the laundry, cleaning the house, and chauffeuring the kids. They love being busy.

If doers feel they are doing all the work, they may express this feeling in brief outbursts of anger or moodiness, but they go right on doing what they do. Sometimes doers even play a complaining game: "Nobody ever helps around here. I always wash the clothes." When someone offers to help, doers turn down the offer and do it themselves. Doers know that only they can do it right. In the complaining game doers may develop another identity, that of the "martyr." In the martyr role, the doing remains constant with the added element of perpetual complaining. The doer is also set up to later become a workaholic.

6. *The Enabler*. This role has been used to describe the person who lives with an alcoholic and does nothing to confront the drinking. The same holds true in sexual addiction. The enabler tolerates inappropriate sexual behavior and does nothing to confront it. Enablers feel they wouldn't have an identity if they weren't somehow related to the addict.

Lies and excuses are the enabler's tools. They like to give the impression their family is "normal." Outsiders may wonder why the enabler puts up with things as they are. The solutions seem so obvious to anyone not so invested or enmeshed in the family—get out! Enablers may have to deal with well-meaning friends who openly offer this solution.

In the Christian community, enablers may seem like saints. We might ask, "How do they put up with that craziness? It takes real faith, courage, and love to live like that!"

7. *The Little Princess/Prince*. The little princess or prince is expected by the family to be warm and wonderful, cute and cuddly, and to exemplify to the world that only a special family could produce such a dream child. This child learns to smile, to dress in the best clothes, and to do little songs and dances at the discretion of parents. The job of the little prince or princess is to entertain and please others.

Whatever feelings may be going on inside, the little princess or prince learns to hide them to always seem happy. These children grow up to be the kind of people everyone likes. They are charming, poised, polite, and graceful. They have charisma. An intuitive observer will sense that the exterior behavior is a false front, but being the little princess or prince, like all the other roles, is learned early and played well at great sacrifice to emotional well-being.

8. *The Saint.* The saint is the family hero who is expected to be perfect in a religious way. The family may have some religious persuasion or none at all, yet the saint will be exemplary of things deep, philosophical, and spiritual. All religious tasks of the family— praying, going to church, reading the Bible, or participating in other religious activities—will be initiated by or performed by the saint.

Saints may be expected to enter a "religious" occupation. Many pastors, priests, nuns, and rabbis followed their families' expectations into the ministry. They may not have done this consciously, but somewhere they felt the directing to be ordained. This may not be the calling of God but the calling of the family. The saint may have other abilities and talents and never get to use them.

Combining Roles. In unhealthy families, more than one person can play the same role. Persons can also switch back and forth between roles. And the same person can play more than one role. In fact, most families are comprised of people playing combinations of roles. The doer and the enabler are frequently combined. Doing all the family functions enables others not to have to do them. The mascot can be combined with any of the other roles. The hero can be great at cracking jokes. The saint can be played in tandem with the hero or the little princess/prince. One of the ways that a saint can learn his or her role is by performing little prince or princess activities at church. Any combination is possible.

Many pastors play the hero-saint-lost child. They are put on a pedestal (the hero); they are expected to be perfectly religious (the saint); and they spend lots of time alone (the lost child). This combination of roles is tragically lonely. When a pastor has committed sexual sins, the hero-saint-lost child role combination prevents him from getting help.

All of us continue to play our roles after we leave our families. At work, we will find that we interact with our bosses and co-workers similarly to the ways we interacted with family members. In church, we play roles learned from childhood. While the pastor plays the hero-saint, many of us play the doers. In marriage we look for partners to play roles that complement ours. A hero, for example, will marry a doer-enabler, someone who will keep things running smoothly while the hero is out collecting accolades.

ADDICTIONS

Unhealthy families are full of addicts of one kind or another. Sexual addicts come from families in which there is at least one other addict present. Since one of the main functions of unhealthy families is to keep feelings buried, many family members must work together to keep them buried. Family members can turn to addictions to accomplish this ongoing burial, since the main function of addiction is to escape or numb feelings.

There are two kinds of addictions: *substance* addiction and *behavioral* addiction. Substance addiction involves ingesting or taking a substance such as drugs or alcohol into your body. Behavior addiction involves repetitively performing behaviors such as sexual activity. See figure 3 for a partial list of these addictions.

Any substance or activity might be addictive. The key is whether or not something has become repetitive in an unmanageable way, is used for the purpose of escaping feelings, and has led or will lead to destructive consequences. Many of the chemicals or behaviors that can be addictive might not be evil in themselves. Sex is a God-given, natural, and beautiful activity. Addictions take place when even normal substances and activities become repeated unmanageably and destructively.

Addictions in families are frequently used as stress management strategies. When you said you were bored, lonely, sad, angry, or afraid (all stressful emotions) did someone ever say to you, "Can I fix you something to eat?" or "Why don't you watch TV," or "Take a good stiff drink, that will cure what ails you." These are invitations to manage stressful feelings with behaviors and sub-stances. These stress management strategies will alter moods or at least take your mind off your feelings. These forms of stress management, particularly if used repeatedly by an impressionable child, can become addictive.

The addicts in a family may not think they are out of control with their behaviors. It is likely, however, that family members feel uncomfortable with them. However, the unspoken family rule overrides any discomfort and translates into, "We don't confront these behaviors because we want to keep things running smoothly. We don't want the outside world to know about our problems."

Family members might also deny their addiction and create elaborate delusions to explain away addictive activity. Some family members may initiate their own addictive behaviors as a way to cope with feelings they can't express or don't recognize, like the pain of seeing one of the family slowly killing him or herself. The spouse of a sex addict, for example, may become an overeater or a workaholic. In many families there are multiple addictions practiced simultaneously as family members slowly die of pain, loneliness, and addiction.

It is in the deep and fertile ground of chaos, dysfunction, silence, and abuse that the seeds of sexual addiction are sown. Sex addicts must begin their recovery by understanding what their families were like. How were the boundaries violated? How were the rules verbally and nonverbally communicated? What roles did they play? What addictions were present and how were they modeled?

These questions may be painful to ask. In fact, as you think about this, a voice inside your head may be saying, "Those things weren't true about my family. We don't talk about that. It wasn't so bad. Don't be critical of my family; after all they really loved me." I invite you to put these internal voices on hold as you read this book in search of solutions to sexual addiction.

HEALTHY FAMILIES

BOUNDARIES
- Flexible
- Care and nurture are provided
- Respect for personal boundaries

RULES
- We talk
- We feel
- We accept our problems
- We honestly evaluate the nature of our problems
- We take responsibility for our own actions
- We ask for help

ROLES
- Interchangeable
- The Hero, Saint, Mascot and Doer are played by each member at appropriate times
- Enabling means caring, encouraging, and affirming
- No Scapegoats, Little Prince/Princess, or Lost Children

HEALTHY CHOICES
- Instead of addictions, family members deal with stress, anxiety, fear, sadness, and anger by making healthy choices to self-nurture and ask for help

HEALTHY NURTURE

EMOTIONAL
- Affirmations are given
- Feelings are accepted
- People are listened to
- Individuality is encouraged

PHYSICAL
- Safety is felt
- Basic needs are provided
- Physical self-care is modeled and taught

SEXUAL
- People's bodies are respected
- Intimacy is modeled and taught
- Sex education is provided

SPIRITUAL
- Personal spirituality is modeled
- Spiritual discipline is taught
- Relationship to God based on love, not fear, is encouraged
- Biblical and theological information and teaching is provided

HEALTHY SHAME

HEALTHY SELF

SELF-CARE
- Makes healthy choices
- Nurtures self
- Has intimate relationships
- Asks for help

EMPOWERMENT
- Recognizes need for God and others
- Affirms self while understanding the unmanageability of one's life
- Discovers God's will for oneself

LOVE, JOY, PEACE

Figure 4: Healthy Families

HEALTHY FAMILIES

Healthy families do exist. Even people who come from unhealthy families may strive to create their own healthy family. Many recovering sex addicts are succeeding in this.

The easiest way to understand a healthy family is to reverse the unhealthy characteristics. Figure 4 takes the family model and substitutes healthy dynamics for unhealthy ones.

In healthy families the cornerstone is healthy boundaries. These are flexible. As the third chapter of Ecclesiastes says, there is a time for everything under God's heaven. In healthy families there is a time for touching and a time not to touch. This depends on the intention of the touch. If it is selfishly or sexually motivated, the boundary needs to be high. If it is respectful and nurturing, the boundary can be crossed. In a healthy family a person has a right to his or her own emotional, physical, sexual, and spiritual privacy. If a person in the family wants to cross this privacy boundary, it can be done for nurturing intentions.

The rules in healthy families become positive prescriptions, not negative prohibitions. We talk and feel, we accept and honestly evaluate our problems, we take responsibility for our own behaviors, and we ask for help when we need it.

Roles are interchangeable. No one person plays them all the time. For example, all members can at times be the hero or the doer. Members share responsibility for getting things done. Achievements and recognitions are passed around. Humor is used in non-shaming ways to have fun and enjoy life. Everyone gets a turn at being the mascot. We are all saints. People share the responsibility for modeling healthy spirituality. Enabling becomes a positive virtue of caring, encouraging, and affirming. There are no scapegoats because everyone takes responsibility for their own behaviors and doesn't blame others. No one gets "lost." Their needs are attended to. Members don't isolate themselves, but seek help when they need it.

Instead of addictions as a way of coping with stress and emotions, members of healthy families are taught how to make healthy choices about expressing feelings, solving problems, and nurturing themselves. Experiencing the full range of emotions is not discouraged. If there have been addicted members of the family, they are in recovery. They model sober behaviors and do the things to take care of themselves that will help keep them healthy.

Emotionally, members are affirmed for who they are and what their talents might be. They are encouraged to talk about and work through feelings which are respected. A parent might say to a child, "You seem angry. Can you talk about that anger?" A person who gets this kind of chance to express anger verbally doesn't need to raise the volume or do something physical in order to be heard or noticed.

There is a feeling of physical safety and positive physical self-care is taught and modeled. Sexually, healthy families respect each other's bodies as being the temple of the Spirit. Intimacy is present between parents. Sexual information is openly and appropriately discussed.

Healthy families worship a loving God. They read and teach Scripture. They practice the spiritual disciplines and celebrate the joy of God's creation. Parents don't just send the kids off to church but are involved themselves.

Such families are full of joy and gladness. They help to create people who have a healthy sense of self. Healthy shame is present, but this means that people honestly know both their God-given talents, their human limitations, and their need for God and for other people. They understand that their lives are unmanageable without God.

Such a healthy self results in personal *empowerment*. Healthy family members have an ability to like themselves and to discover God's will for their lives. Healthy selves are also able to nurture themselves, to do nice things for themselves, to understand what they like, to pursue their interests, and to ask for help when they need it. They are capable of intimate relationships. In short, they will be able to "love others *as* they love themselves."

Such families are wonderful to be a part of. Healthy families prevent the cycle of abuse from being passed down from generation to generation.

7

Family Abuse

Joe and his wife Mary have been fighting about sex for years. Ever since the honeymoon, Joe has demanded it, and Mary usually refuses. Then Joe feels rejected, hurt, and very angry, while Mary feels demeaned, manipulated, and also very angry. Their arguments have become volatile and destructive, and both feel guilty that they can't please each other. They think they have a terrible marriage because their sex life is so empty. Joe is also a sex addict. He masturbates, uses pornography, and goes to prostitutes.

The intensity of this argument is based on old wounds incurred in their families. Joe was emotionally abandoned by his mother, who never had much time for him. In the meantime, Mary was raped by her father between the ages of twelve to sixteen. Therefore when Joe demands sex, Mary is reminded of the trauma of the incest. And when she says no, it reminds Joe of being pushed away from his mother. Joe does not go to a prostitute because he needs sex and can't have it with Mary. Rather, he is searching for the love and nurturing he didn't get from his family.

UNDERSTANDING FAMILY ABUSE

Joe and Mary illustrate why it is so important to understand unhealthy family dynamics. Family abuse is the *damage* or *wounds* done to a member of a family. These wounds will negatively affect this member for the rest of his or her life unless he or she understands them and heals from them. Healing for sexual addiction can only begin when a person comes to a conscious awareness of what happened.

The cycle of abuse is vicious. Most people who abuse have been abused themselves. In many families the trail of abuse extends back for generations. Abuse is one vehicle whereby the "sins of the father" (or the mother) are passed down from one generation to the next.

Christians may wonder if sex addicts aren't just trying to blame their families or their abusers for their behaviors. The fact is that *unrecovered* sex addicts will indeed blame lots of other people, including parents. However, blame for the purpose of blame is unhealthy and in fact violates the commandment to honor mothers and fathers.

Describing abuse is for the purpose of *understanding*, not for the purpose of blaming. Blame implies judgment. Understanding implies healing. Recovering sex addicts seek to understand their abuse so they might heal from it. But they should not use this understanding to blame others for their own behaviors.

To understand the abuse and heal from it, the victim will need to be angry. The victim will also need to confront the parent or other perpetrator about the abuse. Both the anger and the confrontation are meant to heal the victim, not to blame the abuser, and are vital parts of recovering from sexual addiction.

The Old Testament clearly shows that the sins of the parents bring misfortune to future generations (Ex. 20:5) and the sins of the father and mother should not be forgotten (Ps. 109:14). David's sexual sin with Bathsheba left a legacy of sexual problems, including incest and murder.

Understanding abuse allows people to recognize what happened to them and how they cope with it through their addictions. It allows them to understand how painful the abuse was, how frightened they were, how alone they felt, and how angry they are. By acknowledging these feelings and finding healthy ways to express them and cope with them, they can be healed.

To be abused by a parent is an *intensely* powerful feeling.

Powerful feelings lead to powerful coping strategies that can, in themselves, be sinful and self-destructive. People who sin and alienate themselves from God have felt alienated from parental love all of their lives. To change, they must know that at the time of the abuse they did the best they could, that they survived, but that now they can make new choices, including accepting the love of a God who is not like their family members.

By confronting the abuser, the victim accepts how powerfully abusive the experience was and stops the behavior from happening in the future. Otherwise, parents who abuse their children could abuse their grandchildren in the same way.

Victims of abuse need to watch themselves also lest they repeat their parents' mistakes. We all tend to reenact what we have learned. To us, the behavior, no matter how abusive, was "normal"—it was what we knew every day as we were growing up—and we may repeat it without thinking about it.

Sex addicts must look at what happened to them, understand it, allow themselves to feel the pain rather than addictively avoid it, and confront it as a sign that they know it was wrong. This is a process that may take a long time, but it is vital to making healthier choices in the future. When sex addicts make those new choices they *can* break the cycle of sinful abusive behavior and *then* the sins of the parents won't be passed down from generation to generation.

This constructive confrontation does, in fact, *honor* our parents in the way that God commands us. When Nathan confronted David, he honored him enough to seek his restoration. When sex addicts hold parents accountable, they honor them by also seeking restoration. Restoration can only take place when past behaviors aren't repeated and feelings are expressed.

I have divided abuse into four kinds: emotional, physical, sexual, and spiritual (see figure 5). Within these four kinds are two types of abuse: invasion and abandonment. If the boundaries in a family have become too *loose*, the abuse is an *invasion*. Someone's emotional, physical, sexual, or spiritual boundaries have been invaded or crossed. If the boundaries in a family have become too

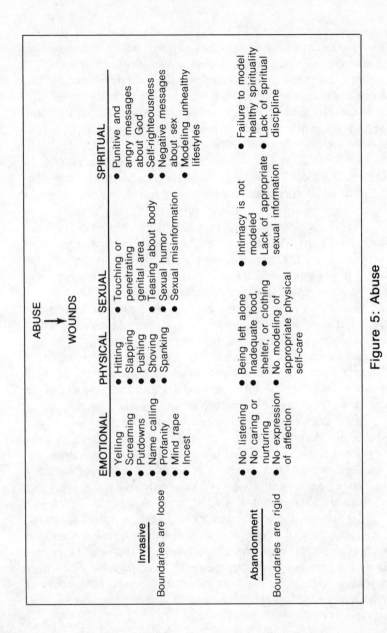

Figure 5: Abuse

rigid, the abuse is an *abandonment*. Someone does not get the love, attention, nurturing, or information they need to thrive.

Pat Carnes found in his research with one thousand sex addicts that ninety-seven percent were emotionally abused, seventy-four percent were physically abused, and eighty-one percent were sexually abused.[1] These figures reveal that abuse plays an important part in the development of sexual addiction. Thus, for sexual addicts to be healed, it is vital for them to understand the abuse they suffered and how it has affected them.

EMOTIONAL ABUSE

A person's emotional boundaries can be *invaded* in several ways. The *first* way is by hearing that they are innately "bad." Perhaps the most obvious way is the yelling and screaming that carries with it the direct verbal message: "You're no good, I hate you, you'll never amount to anything, I regret the day you were born, you're dumb, and you're ugly."

The same messages can be conveyed matter of factly: "It doesn't surprise me that you failed, you've always failed, you might as well not apply to that college, you're not smart enough to get in; you wouldn't dare ask her out, she would never go out with someone like you."

At other times the message is very subtle: "Why didn't you get better grades? Your brother always did; Why are you dating that guy? He's a real loser." Some of us are familiar with a look from our parents, a frown, a slump of the shoulders, a pointing of the finger, a tone of the voice, or a sigh of despair.

All of these messages are abusive. They are the result of misplaced anger inappropriately expressed and not intended for constructive criticism or discipline. They are abusive because they create long-lasting and damaging wounds in the victim.

The *second* invasive way people can be emotionally abused is to be convinced that their thoughts and feelings are "bad." "Mind rape" is a rather harsh but appropriate description of this kind of abuse in which a person is not allowed to have his or her feelings.

Statements such as "Please don't feel that way" or anger statements like "That's a stupid way to feel" or "Cheer up and get your act together" are examples of mind rape. Family members are encouraged to suppress feelings so that it will help someone else: "It hurts me when you're sad" or "You frighten me when you're angry" or "I worry when you worry" or "If Dad knew you felt that way, he'd die."

Another common message is "You don't *need* to feel that way." This kind of mind rape is based on minimizing and is often accompanied with reasons why the victim doesn't need to feel that way. Solutions may even be offered: "You don't need to feel that way because you could do this to solve your problem." When family members are tempted to be happy, proud, or excited, they might be encouraged to suppress even these positive feelings as a way to avoid conceit. They might also feel lonely because no one else in the family knows how to experience these feelings.

Finally, mind rape can occur when people are convinced they are not mature for feeling the way they do. One of the earliest messages many of us receive is, "Big girls/boys don't cry." Along the way we may be encouraged to "grow up," "act your age," or "stop being a baby."

Christians add mini-sermons to their messages with the theme, "A mature Christian wouldn't feel that way." We might be convinced our salvation is not intact if we feel sad, anxious, or angry. At my grandmother's funeral the minister convinced us all to stop crying as a way to reflect our Christian belief in Grandma's salvation. While I believe I will indeed see her again, telling us not to cry at her funeral robbed us of our ability to grieve. I call this "religious mind rape."

In mind rape the content of the message is often correct, but the timing is inappropriate and is designed to stop people from feeling. The intentions may be loving, but the "mind rapist" is uncomfortable or inept with emotions and avoids that discomfort by stopping someone else from having them.

Mind rape occurs when someone does not listen to or accept the validity of someone else's feelings. The result is that the victim begins to think it is bad, immature, irresponsible, weak, unfaithful, or otherwise unacceptable to have those feelings. But somewhere inside these feelings remain buried.

Later on in life victims of mind rape may have similar feelings to the ones suppressed when they were small. As a result, they will continue to hide their feelings and to look for ways to numb or escape them altogether, while at the same time condemning themselves for not being able to feel. To the outsider, abuse victims seem to hide their feelings intentionally. That is not the case. Abuse victims are either too numb, too afraid, or too ashamed to talk about feelings. They think, "If you really knew me, you would hate me." They have an extremely hard time being honest with their feelings.

A *third* kind of invasive emotional abuse occurs when a parent creates a marriage-like relationship with a child. The lonely parent may have a bad marriage or be a single parent due to divorce or death, and therefore turns to the child as a special friend, buddy, confidant, and companion. The child learns to listen to, accompany, and nurture the parent. What the parent likes, the child likes. What the parent does, the child does. This is called *covert emotional incest*.[2]

This may seem like a very special relationship, for the child gets to do privileged things with one of his or her parents. He or she may feel extremely powerful because even at a young age the parent is sharing feelings that are not told to anyone else.

The child, however, does not get his or her feelings listened to, needs met, or interests and abilities encouraged. If Dad wants him to be a baseball player, that's what he'll be. If Mom wants her to go to law school, that's what she'll do. The result? Victims lose touch with who they are and what they like. Their identity is made up of what their parent thinks, likes, and feels.

One man told me about his girlfriend, who called her mother constantly, spent excessive amounts of time with her, and even oriented some of their dates around her. "Do you think I should marry this girl?" he asked me.

"No," I replied. "It would be a case of bigamy. She's already married to her mother."

Emotional incest can exist between a father and son, father and daughter (daddy's little girl), mother and son, or mother and daughter. The other parent is excluded from the relationship, sometimes in obvious ways ("Your father's never home") and sometimes in less obvious ways ("Why don't just you and I go to the game? Mom doesn't like baseball anyway"). The message is clear. The other parent has some negative characteristic that makes it imperative that the incestuous parent and child "stick together."

People who are victims of emotional incest grow up with a voice inside them that always wonders, "What would mom/dad think about this?" They don't know how to nurture, like, or care for themselves, but they do know how to take care of mom or dad. As they become adults they may turn this need to care for one parent into a need to care for others. Just as their identity as children was formed by how well they took care of their parent, their identity as adults may be formed by how *much* they can take care of others. Many people in the ministry and other helping professions are emotional incest victims.

The opposite of invasive emotional abuse is emotional *abandonment*. This type of abuse is just as devastating. Victims of abandonment have experienced someone *leaving* them emotionally. This person may be physically present, but they don't talk, share themselves, or listen to the family member needing emotional nurturing. They seem cold, distant, or unconcerned.

If this family member does care, he or she is not able to express it, and family members are held off at arm's length. Parents and others who perpetrate this type of abuse may also be abuse victims and think no one needs their emotional care. Whatever the case, they don't know how to give of themselves in an emotionally nurturing way and their children feel abandoned.

In the emotional incest described earlier, the parent who commits incest usually forms an alliance with the child against the other parent. If the other parent does nothing to prevent this or even goes along with it, this is abandonment. The very same child can be abandoned by one parent and emotionally abused by the other.

When a young child is emotionally abandoned, a very deep emotional void is created. The child may not be consciously aware of it but does know a profound loneliness and longing for affection. The child may have this feeling even when many people are around and trying to offer affection. However, the love and nurture of a parent can never be replaced, and nothing can fill that void. Sexual addiction may be an attempt to find love and nurturing care, but it is a misplaced search and never works.

PHYSICAL ABUSE

Physical abuse that is *invasive* occurs when a person's body is hit, slapped, shoved, or pushed, or when some other form of physical violence takes place. Children, spouses, even grandparents are likely to be victims of physical harm at the hands of a family member. Physical abuse occurs when one person is angry and tries to control another. Spanking done in anger and not for the purpose of discipline can be physically abusive. Victims of physical abuse are continually frightened and feel they don't have control of their physical safety.

Family members who witness violence can also be victims. If a child sees his mother being physically abused by his father, the effects can be just as damaging as if the child was also hit. Many Viet Nam veterans who were not physically injured or who never injured others still experience many symptoms of chronic anxiety and depression.

This condition is called Post Traumatic Stress Disorder (PTSD). People with PTSD learn how to "dissociate" their minds and emotions from the reality around them. They let the mind leave their body and go someplace else, to other thoughts or safe imaginary places. Certain behaviors or chemicals may be used to dissociate and thereby become the seed of many addictions. Many sex addicts who were physically abused suffer from PTSD.

Physical abandonment abuse occurs when basic physical needs are not met. Inadequate shelter, food, clothing, and medical care are not provided. A more subtle form of physical abandonment occurs when children are not taught to take care of themselves physically. Children need to learn how to go to bed on time, eat nutritious foods, brush their teeth, take care of personal hygiene, and exercise. When self-care is not modeled or taught, abandonment takes place.

Physical abandonment may also take place when a child is left alone, particularly when very small. The child may develop a sense of not being physically safe even though no physical danger is present. When both parents choose to work outside the home, possibly leaving a child to care for himself, he may feel physically abandoned.

SEXUAL ABUSE

Estimates vary greatly, but it is believed that twenty-five to thirty-three percent of all women have at some time in their life been sexually abused. While we used to assume that it was rare for a man to have been sexually abused, we now believe that ten to fifteen percent of men have been abused in this way. How can we have accurate figures about this problem when it is such a difficult one to admit? Sexual abuse is such a damaging problem that many people repress the ugliness of the experience, don't remember it, and might even deny that they are victims.

Invasive sexual abuse involves having the genital areas touched or penetrated by someone who holds either physical or emotional power over the victim. As a result, victims lose the sense that they have control of their bodies and live in perpetual fear of being "invaded" or of something harmful happening. Like physical abuse victims, they may also suffer the symptoms of Post Traumatic Stress Disorder. As adults they may have great difficulty with normal sexual activity. Many may not remember the childhood experience and do not even know what's wrong with them. This can cause great shame and confusion. "What's wrong with me? Why am I so afraid? Why can't I be normal sexually?" Many people, in fact, ask these questions even if they do remember the sexual abuse.

Often the sexual abuser is a trusted person. As a result, the victim may have difficulty trusting. If the abuser was a man, men may not be trusted. If a female abuser is involved, women will not be trusted. If the abuser was a professional, authority may not be respected. If the abuser was a pastor, God himself might not be trusted.

There are more subtle forms of invasive sexual abuse. Kissing, hugging, touching, lap sitting, and tickling may have the same effect as more direct sexual abuse. The victim will have a sense that the physical contact is not for the purpose of healthy nurturing but rather for the sexual gratification of the other person.

Many people have at one time or another slept in the same bedroom or even the same bed with one of their parents. Sometimes it is because the child was frightened by the dark or a thunderstorm. But it may be that the parent is emotionally or sexually lonely. At any rate, it is not necessarily wrong for a child to sometimes sleep in the parents' bedroom. The distinction centers on *why* the child is there. If the child feels uncomfortable with it, it is abusive.

A parent may walk into the bedroom or the bathroom when a child is getting dressed, bathing, or using the bathroom for its normally intended purpose. This becomes abusive, even if it involves the parent of the same sex, when the child enters adolescence, because it teaches children that they have no control over their environment or their privacy. Feelings of shame or embarrassment result. Later in life they may become protective and unable to experience their body without those feelings of shame.

Another form of invasive abuse occurs when children are teased about their body, their development, or any sexual or romantic feelings that they have. A woman told me that her father announced at a Thanksgiving gathering of her entire family that she had started menstruating. He kidded her that she needed to start watching out for boys and it was his job to protect her. This amazingly insensitive comment had more to do with the father's discomfort with sex than it did with his fear of boys in his daughter's life, and he was passing that discomfort on to his daughter. It was abusive. It created wounds. The women telling me the story had tears in her eyes, and she was seventy years old.

Our families are bad enough; our peers can be worse. Many of us were teased mercilessly about sexuality and our bodies by our "friends." This teasing is extremely painful and also reflects incorrect sexual information.

Our entire culture sexually abuses us through the messages it sends to us on TV, movies, radio, or magazines. We innocently take in misinformation while we wait to pay for our groceries. The sexual messages are myriad, and few of them are based on the Word of God.

The other side of invasive sexual abuse is *abandonment* sexual abuse. Ask yourself, what messages would you receive about sex if your family never talked about it? Would it be hard for you to imagine, biologically, how you even got here if your parents never touched each other, seemed affectionate, or mentioned the word *sex*? Would you feel afraid about your physical and sexual development if you had no one to talk to? For example, junior highers take a shower after physical education. Do you remember that first shower, and being naked in front of your peers? Instead of physical education this experience becomes a class in comparative anatomy. Whom did you talk to about whatever feelings you had?

The effect of this abandonment is that people grow up believing that feelings are unique to them. Since no one else has ever talked to them about normal sexual feelings they assume their sexual feelings are abnormal. They may even start to interpret their normal sexual curiosity as perverted if they can't compare it to others and discover that it is normal. They may become afraid of their sexual feelings. They might infer that since sex is never talked about, it must be bad. Sex addicts have extremely distorted and fearful ideas about sexuality. They don't think they can talk to anyone about it. Abandonment sexual abuse will prevent the adult sex addict from getting the help so desperately needed.

SPIRITUAL ABUSE

We were having coffee at the home of some Christian friends when their three-year-old daughter, who was playing on the banister, fell off, bumped her head, and began to cry. The mother put her arms around her and said, "There now, big girls don't cry." Then she said, "I wonder if Jesus wanted you sliding down that banister? I think that if he did he wouldn't have let you bump your head."

Often parents will discipline their children by warning them of the consequences that God might send. It may be theologically correct to teach the consequences of sinful behavior, but there is a way to do so that emphasizes the love of God rather than his wrath. Would a wrathful God have sent his Son to die for us? Yet many Christians of many different denominations have been raised with an image of a strict and vengeful God.

Invasive spiritual abuse convinces people they are evil and do only sinful things, making them so afraid of God's anger and disapproval that they look for rigid, black and white answers. Without the right answers, they won't do the right things, and God will be angry. People subject to this kind of abuse also make sure that they read the Bible and pray—not to nurture themselves spiritually, but to appease God and avoid punishment. They may also learn to repress feelings that they have been taught are "un-Christian," such as anger or fear. This form of abuse is what I call "religious mind rape."

Invasive spiritual abuse might also teach us very negative attitudes about sexuality. Instead of celebrating God's great gift of marital sexuality, we might have learned that sex is dirty, disgusting, awful, or only for the purpose of procreation and not to be enjoyed. The silence of the church about sexual issues contributes to the feeling that if the church doesn't talk about sex, it must be bad.

There is even the feeling that to be truly spiritual one should avoid sex altogether. The Catholic Church has promulgated this idea by telling their clergy that to truly serve God they must be celibate. Celibacy is a gift of service that can be given to God, but it is incorrect to equate marriage with a lower form of spirituality.

This fear of sex affects sex addicts in two ways. First, it encourages them to keep quiet about their problem. If they have committed sexual sins and know the church has negative and judgmental attitudes about sexuality, they will be even more ashamed. Sexual sinners should feel guilty and make amends for what they have done, but an overwhelming sense of personal shame and a fear that God or the church will punish them may lead them to be totally silent. As a result, they may never get help.

Second, negative attitudes about sex make it a tantalizing "forbidden fruit." This makes the pursuit of sex a dangerous and therefore even more stimulating activity. Sex becomes exciting for both its pleasure and its danger. Both qualities can be addicting by allowing the addict to escape feelings.

This dynamic has led Dr. Carnes to conclude that to a sex addict, "For sex to be good, it has to be bad."[3] For sex to be exciting or pleasurable, it has to be forbidden. Often, sex addicts are attracted to "bad" sex because of their family background. If they have been sexually abused at the same time they are told not to be promiscuous or to avoid sex, they are taught that sex is hurtful and emotionally painful. A child in this situation may think, "Dad tells me not to be sexual, but he does have sex with me. That really hurts, but it must be all right since it is Dad doing it." This child is programmed to look for painful sexual relationships later in life.

These dynamics also condition a person to be rebellious about sex. "My parents say I shouldn't. My church says I shouldn't. Yet they have abused or abandoned me. I'm angry. What does God care? I'm going to be sexual anyway." Whether verbalized or unconscious, this thought has the power to lead a person into rebellious sexual encounters.

My own informal research confirms what other sociologists of religion suggest: People from rigidly religious homes that teach negative messages about sex are more likely to have difficulty with sexual addiction. Several prostitutes have told me that they are glad to see Christian conventions come to town because their "business" will increase. Hotel chains have studied the use of in-room TV pornography and report that usage increases during Christian conventions. And I have consulted with evangelical churches where affairs in the congregation were rampant, and one in which wife-swapping was raging in one of the adult Sunday school classes.

Besides invasive spiritual abuse, there is also the spiritual abuse of abandonment, when the parents do not model a healthy spirituality. Such parents may be pillars of the church and pay lipservice to Christian values without living them at home. They may push church attendance and religious practices on the child without taking them seriously themselves. Worse, they may preach religious values but be violating them, even going so far as to commit other forms of abuse. This hypocrisy destroys trust. When people are abandoned spiritually, they will not have resources to turn to when they get into trouble. Many sex addicts are completely devoid of a healthy sense of spirituality and are alienated from the church because of all the fear and negativity described above. One of the major challenges of recovery will be for them to come to a healthy sense of spirituality.

THE WOUNDED SELF AND SHAME

When children have been abused, they become wounded emotionally, sexually, spiritually, and sometimes physically (see figure 6). They were too small and too helpless to defend themselves against these injuries. What are children to think about themselves when they are being invaded or abandoned? They come to a very logical conclusion: "If this is happening to me, I must be bad, because bad people are punished." Or "If no one loves me, it must be because I am bad. Good people are loved."

This woundedness leads to a very deep feeling called *shame*. There is a *healthy* sense of shame. As John Bradshaw said in his book, *Healing the Shame that Binds You*, shame in itself is not bad.[4] Healthy shame recognizes that all people have both abilities and limitations. Healthy shame teaches us that we need others, that we can't exist on our own and always take care of ourselves. It is part of the human condition and points a person toward a healthy dependence on others and on God.

Abuse victims, however, have internalized this sense of natural shame and believe themselves to be completely worthless and shameful. Healthy shame expresses the conviction that human beings are not able to earn their own salvation and that they must

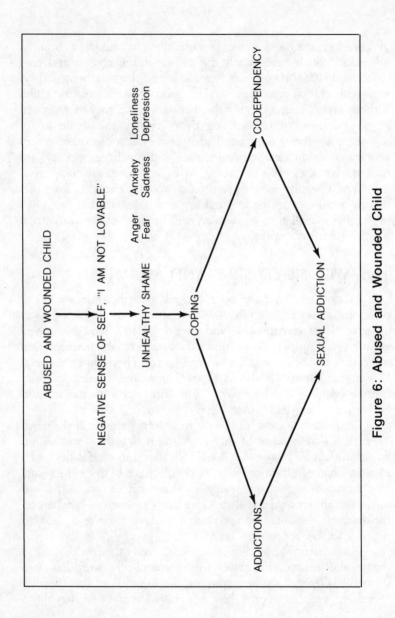

Figure 6: Abused and Wounded Child

depend on God. Unhealthy shame tells people to believe that they do not deserve God's salvation and probably won't be able to earn it. This kind of shame also tells people that they have an evil nature and that there is no goodness inside.

Shame is not the same thing as guilt. Dr. Sandra Wilson, author of several books on codependency and shame, gives the best distinction: "Guilt is when we know we've made mistakes. Shame is when we feel we *are* a mistake."[5]

Unhealthy shame prevents people from giving themselves any kind of affirmation. Nothing that they do, no victories won, no accomplishments of any kind will convince them that they are good. They may even go to church and hear the Word of God, they may believe in Christ, they may know him in their head, but they don't *feel* him in their heart.

Unhealthy shame is the central feeling of the abused and wounded child. Attached to this core feeling are other feelings (see figure 6). The abandoned child will feel lonely and sad. The abused child will feel anxious and fearful.

Another feeling attached to shame is anger. Although abuse victims believe they deserved the abuse, another part of them is deeply angry about the abuse. Yet they don't allow themselves to feel, much less experience, this anger. It lies buried and festers, and sometimes it reveals itself in addictive behavior. The anger will leak out somehow no matter how hard a person tries to repress it.

Sexual addicts have four core beliefs about themselves:

1. I am a bad, unworthy person.
2. No one will love me as I am.
3. No one can take care of my needs but me.
4. Sex is my most important need.[6]

Sexual addicts believe that sexual activity is the only way to meet their need for love and nurturing. How does a sexual addict cope with this need for love and with their deep sense of shame? That is the topic of the next chapter.

8.

How Sex Addicts Cope with Abuse

Sex addicts come from families in which the dynamics are mostly unhealthy and abusive. The abuse has led them to feel shame in unhealthy ways. Many of the strategies they learn to cope with abuse and shame have been modeled to them by their parents and other family members.

The strategies sex addicts employ for dealing with abuse and shame can be divided into two very broad categories. First, they will try to *escape* the feelings of unhealthy shame. Second, they will search in others for the approval that they can't give themselves and thereby become *codependent*.

ESCAPE

Because sex addicts can't tolerate painful feelings, they seek to escape the feelings through sexual activity. Research has shown that sexual activity and sexual fantasy can alter brain chemistry and produce profound feelings of pleasure.[1] This can be a beautiful experience between two committed people. Sex addicts, however, are in the business of altering their brain chemistry, and thereby their mood, all the time. They use sex like a drug to produce a high. As the disease progresses, the sex addict cares less and less who the sexual partner is. The main pursuit is the high. If they can't find a partner, masturbation will give them a "quick fix."

Sometimes the danger inherent in promiscuous sexual activity will produce adrenalin that can also be addicting. Sex addicts may pursue dangerous sexual liaisons, such as men who have sex with married women when her husband is due home shortly. They get a high from the sex, from a new partner, and from the danger. In their excitement, they temporarily forget their anxieties, fears, sadness, loneliness, or anger.

Sexual activity is not the only addiction that sex addicts might use to escape. Addiction of all kinds can come into play. Any of them can be dangerously pursued and therefore "exciting," giving addicts a rush of adrenalin.

The more profoundly abused a person has been, the more likely this person will be to have multiple addictions. For example, roughly forty percent of all sex addicts that Golden Valley Health Center has treated are also alcoholics.[2] A sex addict may also need to be in recovery from addictions to alcohol, drugs, and other substances or behaviors.

Escape and mood alteration is not the only reason certain chemicals or behaviors, like sex, become addictive. Another possibility is that they are used as a *reward*. Sex addicts believe that no one else is going to take care of them, so when they feel they have been "good" or done something well, they reward themselves with addictive activity.

CODEPENDENCY

The other route to dealing with unhealthy shame is to find approval outside of the self. An ashamed person doesn't like herself and must find someone who does.

Codependency is an addiction to approval and any behaviors done to get approval. Sexual addicts believe one way to get approval is through sexual activity. They might think that people willing to be sexual with them must like them. If sex addicts are to heal, they must learn how to find approval in healthy ways. It is vital, then, to fully understand codependency.

Codependency originally referred to people in a significant relationship with an alcoholic. The alcoholic is dependent on alcohol, and the codependent is dependent on the alcoholic. A codependent's attachment to and need for approval is so uncontrollable that she can't leave or take care of herself despite the drinking and abusive behaviors that go along with alcoholism.

Codependency is often used to describe anyone addicted to another person. Most codependents were abandoned as children and grow up to be *deathly* afraid of someone leaving them again. Codependents will completely sacrifice their needs and interests if that is what it takes to please the person whose approval they so desperately need. This sacrifice will bring with it a great cost. Codependents will work so hard to get others to like them they burn themselves out and get tired and depressed.

Codependents are so afraid of someone leaving that they develop great anxieties. Preoccupied about what they can do to maintain another's approval, they neglect other important matters in life.

Codependents may believe that people will like them if they have enough money, a nice house, a fancy car, a powerful job, or the right educational degrees. Some ministers are "ordained codependents," believing that people will like them only if they are ministers. Codependents busy themselves, sometimes feverishly, trying to get ahead in life. Sometimes success will give them short bursts of approval and they feel good for a short time, but it doesn't last. Then they need another fix and get busy again to earn it.

Codependents use many ways to try to keep a person with them. Sometimes they don't need the person to like them so much as they simply need them to be there. They might do countless acts of service, sacrificing their own time and interests, to please another. They can be endless caretakers.

Sex addicts who are codependents need lots of sex in order to like themselves. They think sex is their most important need. Through sex, they get the admiration and the nurturing they are starved for. They might employ codependent strategies not only to keep a person with them, but also to get sex from them.

To all of Helen's friends her husband, Harry, seemed like the model man. He was always doing things for her, buying her things, bringing her flowers, and helping with household chores. Her time was his time. What she wanted he wanted. Harry was such a great husband, how could she refuse him sexually? She was shocked one day when she found a stack of pornography in his closet. Harry was a codependent sex addict continually trying to "earn" sexual favors from his wife.

Codependent strategies seldom work for very long, although they may bring temporary relief from the pain and anxieties of being abandoned. Usually codependency compels a person to pursue sexual activities that are sinful and thereby shameful. Codependency temporarily relieves shame but in the long term it only serves to increase it. Many people go back and forth between a desperate search for approval and a need to escape the feeling that they never really get it. This is an endless, vicious cycle.

Sexual addiction is an attempt to manage shame by employing *both* the strategies of escape and codependency simultaneously. Sexual activity becomes both an escape and a search for approval at the same time.

Now add up all of the dynamics that I have written about in this section (see figure 7). Sexual addiction is powerful because it attempts to manage the unhealthy sense of shame that an unhealthy family has created.

Sex is an attractive activity, not just because it is a major lustful tool that the devil uses to lead people astray, but also because it can be medication for the wounds of childhood. As such it is a *survival strategy*. This strategy avoids short-term pain for a slower death. Just as a cocaine addict will long for the medication of the next high, a sex addict will do the same.

Anyone who has ever been frustrated with a sex addict because he or she won't stop acting out needs to remember that sexual activity, at least in the mind of addicts, has allowed them to survive pain. It is not that sex addicts don't want to give up sex. It is not that they are terrible, sinful, immoral people. It is because they can't give up the coping strategies they believe have kept them alive for years.

When a spouse, a friend, a pastor, or a counselor asks a sex

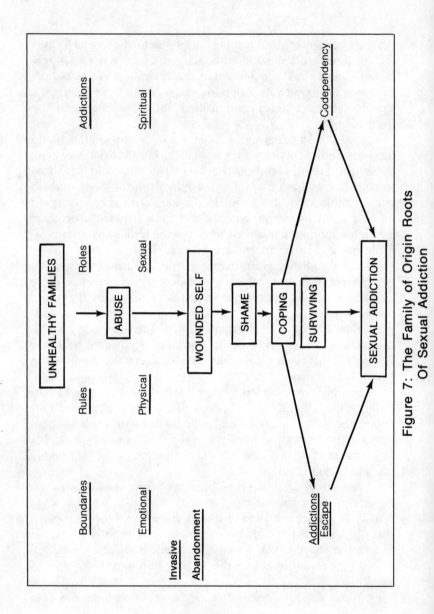

Figure 7: The Family of Origin Roots Of Sexual Addiction

addict to stop acting out sexually, the sex addict hears this message at one level and agrees with it. Yet there is a simultaneous voice inside that says, "If I give this up, I will die. The pain is too intense. I can't stand it." Another voice, at another level, quickly follows: "Why should I give this up? It is the only thing that I do for myself. No one else takes care of me." This last voice is the voice of the abandonment victim and says, often in anger, "Don't tell me to stop. People have been denying me my needs for years. Who will take care of me?"

When we seek to help a sex addict stop, we are dealing with an adult who agrees with us and a wounded child who doesn't. If our logic and strategies are only aimed at the adult who agrees with us already, we will fail.

RELIGIOUS ADDICTION AND CODEPENDENCY

When Dan was a boy his parents made him go to church so that he could avoid going to hell. Dan was emotionally abused by his dad, who never affirmed anything that he did. Now, while Dan's successful law practice brought him praise, he didn't enjoy it and didn't like himself. Lately, he had turned to visiting prostitutes more and more.

Dan was also a pillar in his church. He served on many committees, and as president of the church council he attended almost every function. He also taught Sunday school and sang in the choir. The pastor called him his "right-hand man" and didn't know what he would do without Dan.

Yet when I talked to Dan he confessed that he never felt satisfied and always felt guilty. He looked constantly for more religious activity to help him feel better. He told me he had decided to quit his law practice and go to seminary at age forty-three. Maybe becoming a pastor would satisfy him.

Dan did go to seminary, but he was arrested for soliciting prostitution. Eventually, he went to treatment and returned to his law practice, where he works primarily with sex offenders. He discovered that he was called to ministry by guilt and his religious addiction and not by God.

Religious addiction involves the notion that there is a *formula* that will lead to approval, happiness, and success. Sexual addicts believe that if they can get the formula right, their lust will be taken away.

The danger of religious addiction is that the effort or the *practice of religion* becomes more important than any hoped-for result. Being religiously busy becomes more important than an intimate and nurturing relationship with God. Sex addicts have been impaired in their families and do not know how to have healthy intimacy. How can they know intimacy with a God who is called Father when they have not learned healthy intimacy in other relationships?

Jesus encountered religious addiction. In Mark 2:23–28 the incredulous Pharisees questioned him about his disciples breaking the Law by plucking ears of grain on the Sabbath. Jesus reminds them of how King David ate bread from the high altar which, lawfully, was meant only for the priests. Jesus then goes on to say that the Sabbath was made for man, not man for the Sabbath. We do not obey laws in order to please and pacify God. Rather, laws are made for our protection and to teach us how to nurture ourselves and have a healthy relationship with God and others.

The Pharisees were religiously addicted. The practice of religion was more important to them than people and their spiritual needs. The *rigidity* of their religiously addicted thinking prevented the Pharisees from experiencing Jesus as the Messiah.

Religious addiction occurs when we, like the Pharisees, use repetitive religious behaviors to get the formula right in order to feel happy, escape our feelings, and avoid intimacy. Religious addicts think that if they read the Bible one hour a day, two hours would be better. If they go to church twice a week, three times would be more productive. Memorizing one hundred Scripture verses is not as good as one thousand. Serving on one committee is not as good as on five.

Religiously addicted persons create a false sense of security in themselves. They believe that the more they do the better God will like them. In most churches, they also get lots of affirmation for their hard work and extreme effort.

Religious addiction becomes a religious workaholism. The work, in itself, becomes an escape. Work takes lots of thought and energy. It creates its own excitement and adrenalin which distracts the addict from other feelings, however painful. The amount of work may even create "great things" like new church buildings, higher budgets, or more members. There is an excitement to the fruits of this labor. Yet for sex addicts, it is merely another escape.

Since the fix is only a temporary one, more and more religious activity will be needed in order to maintain it. This is the tolerance factor. More and more of the same behavior is needed to sustain the high. Many religious addicts burn themselves out, perhaps even leaving the church to escape their endless cycle of activity. If they don't leave, they might stay around and become resentful that they are the only ones who ever seem to do anything.

Ultimately, religious addicts will be depressed that their activity hasn't produced the happiness they thought it would. Sexual addicts don't achieve freedom from their lust and sexual behaviors and can become very disillusioned with God and religion. I know countless numbers of sex addicts who have left the church for these reasons.

Work and the excitement and adrenalin of it are one form of escape for a religious addict. This achieves the effect of *avoiding* pain. There are also religious ways to *alter* mood. Mood-altering experiences are not unique to cults or eastern religions. The music, the rituals, the repetitive prayers or readings, and the somber or celebrative atmospheres of church may have a mood-altering effect. Christians might say, "They are supposed to make us feel better and help us to be closer to God." But an addict does not use them for relationship, but to alter mood and avoid relationship. To a religious addict, worship can be an ecstatic experience in which they get "carried away." They get carried *away* from relationship with God, not toward it.

These forms of religious expression are not addictive in

themselves. Religious addicts allow the jubilance or the soothing nature of certain religious styles to create what is, in effect, a trancelike state in order to help them avoid what they currently feel. It is much the same as putting music in your stereo not as an expression of how you're feeling but as a way of altering your feeling. You may feel lousy, so you put on some happy or joyous music to make you feel differently. This isn't bad in itself, but if done all the time to always avoid feelings, it could be addictive.

When the formula is working right, the religious addict will indeed begin to feel rather "good." Don't confuse this feeling with a feeling of peace. It is not that. It is based on temporarily avoiding the truly painful feelings inside.

A sexual addict *craves* this experience of being and feeling "good." Religious addiction serves them as a form of escape. In spite of the terribly sinful things that they are doing, they can have a temporary "fix" of feeling like they are not sinful, but rather are spiritual people.

An interesting feature of religious addiction is that it will cause others in the church to think that sexual addicts are actually spiritual people. If their sexual sinfulness ever becomes public, it will surprise those same people because it seems so out of character, a paradox. Christians may ask, "How could she have done those things?" They may find themselves getting angry at the "hypocrite." What they are actually experiencing is a challenge to their faith. If people have committed sexual sin themselves, discovering it in others makes them uncomfortable, for it reminds them of what they have done. It is easier to blame others and avoid them than it is to look at themselves. Often, when a person rejects and judges a sex addict's sinful behavior, he is himself guilty of sexual addiction.

In combination with religious addiction, codependency can lead a sex addict to a maddening pace of activity and caring work. This is one reason why so many of them are, in fact, pillars of the church. Many have been looked to as shining examples of faith.

Sex addict codependents have heard the commandment, "You shall love your neighbor" (Lev. 19:18). But they never hear the second part of that passage, "as yourself," for they do not know how to love themselves. Codependents in the church have retranslated this verse into: "Love others because you would have them love you." However, since sex addicts don't love themselves, they are unable to love others. Instead of loving others, they do things for others hoping that others will love them. Others must love them because they can't love themselves.

Christian charity and work done as the result of codependent thinking is not in *response* to God's love, as it should be, but is an attempt to *earn* God's love. Codependent thinking leads to a theology of salvation by works, and not salvation by faith. The challenge to a sexually addicted codependent is to learn that he or she doesn't have to burn out trying to earn God's or anyone else's nurture. It is while we were yet sinners that Christ died for us. His love does not need to be either earned or deserved—it is a gift freely offered.

Shame creates codependency and prevents many people, including sex addicts, from accepting the gift of Jesus Christ. A sexually addicted codependent will think, "If God sent Jesus to die for sins, it wasn't for mine; they are too sexually terrible for even Jesus to imagine." When they think like this, their sexual behaviors remain the secret sin that not even Christ can heal.

Part III

Healing the Wounds of Sexual Addiction

9.

The Twelve Steps: A Tool for Healing

There is much that Christians can do to heal the wounds of sexual addiction. This chapter describes the process of individual recovery in the tradition of the Twelve Steps. Sex addicts now use the Twelve Steps to begin their process of healing, and many are for the first time achieving sexual sobriety.

TWELVE STEP FELLOWSHIPS

The Twelve Steps (see figure 8) are principles developed by Bill Wilson, founder of Alcoholics Anonymous. He expanded them from a list used by the Oxford Group, an informal evangelistic movement popular in many denominations in the earlier part of this century.

In the late 1970s several groups around the country began seeing sexually compulsive behavior as an addiction to sex. Like alcoholics, those who suffered sexual addictions began to meet and found that in their fellowship they began getting well. Sex and Love Addicts Anonymous was formed in Boston, while addicts in Minneapolis started Sex Addicts Anonymous, and addicts in Los Angeles founded Sexaholics Anonymous.

These groups have developed hundreds of chapters around the country, and all of them borrow from the Twelve-Step tradition of Alcoholics Anonymous. For example, the first step of S.A.A. is, "We admitted that we were powerless over our compulsive sexual behavior and that our lives had become unmanageable." All of these groups developed their own guidebooks to tell stories of recovering sex addicts and explain the principles of the fellowship. Their meetings, with some variations, are very similar to A.A. meetings.

Since these programs are based on principles of anonymity, it is not important to identify who actually started the groups. Much like the early history of A.A., the growth of sexual addiction fellowships has been very quiet and secretive, and the groups have often met in churches.

In the early 1980s Dr. Patrick Carnes first began writing about sexually compulsive behavior as sexual addiction. His book, *Out of the Shadows*, has become the unofficial "big book" for many sex addicts. Dr. Carnes and others have published other books which shed new light on sexually addictive behavior.[1]

In most of the Twelve-Step fellowships, the word *recovery* refers to the process of practicing the steps. A person who is "recovering" has at least embraced the first step, "We admitted that we were powerless over our sexual addiction and that our lives had become unmanageable." To be "in recovery" means that a person is going to meetings, has a sponsor, is working on the steps, is perhaps getting counseling, and is sexually sober or trying to be sober.

The word *recovery* may be frightening to Christians who are wary of cults or any substitute for true spirituality. It often seems that twelve-step groups are a false religion. We are especially bothered by the use of "Higher Power" instead of God or Jesus Christ in the Twelve Steps. However, we must accept that any movement, including twelve-step groups and Christianity, are full of sinners, self-righteous types, and hypocrites.

In the early days of their recovery, sex addicts are going to embrace as a miracle anything that seems to work. They will talk about it in glowing terms in order to prove to themselves that they belong to something truly wonderful. Shame produces the need to believe that this is the only answer and they have finally found it.

However, the Twelve Steps is not *the* answer. They certainly do not attempt to replace Christian principles, but are *one* answer that seems to work. The Twelve Steps as a process are a tool, a form

Figure 8: The Twelve Steps of A.A.

1. We admitted we were powerless over (alcohol)—that our lives had become unmanageable.

2. Came to believe that a Power greater than ourselves could restore us to sanity.

3. Made a decision to turn our will and our lives over to the care of God *as we understood Him.*

4. Made a searching and fearless moral inventory of ourselves.

5. Admitted to God, to ourselves, and to another human being the exact nature of our wrongs.

6. Were entirely ready to have God remove all these defects of character.

7. Humbly asked Him to remove our shortcomings.

8. Made a list of all persons we had harmed, and became willing to make amends to them all.

9. Made direct amends to such people wherever possible, except when to do so would injure them or others.

10. Continued to take personal inventory, and when we were wrong, promptly admitted it.

11. Sought through prayer and meditation to improve our conscious contact with God *as we understood Him,* praying only for knowledge of His will for us and the power to carry that out.

12. Having had a spiritual awakening as the result of these steps, we tried to carry this message to alcoholics, and to practice these principles in all our affairs.

Figure 9: The Twelve Traditions of A.A.

1. Our common welfare should come first; personal recovery depends upon A.A. unity.

2. For our group purpose there is but one ultimate authority—a loving God as He may express Himself in our group conscience. Our leaders are but trusted servants; they do not govern.

3. The only requirement for A.A. membership is a desire to stop drinking.

4. Each group should be autonomous except in matters affecting other groups or A.A. as a whole.

5. Each group has but one primary purpose—to carry its message to the alcoholic who still suffers.

6. An A.A. group ought never endorse, finance, or lend the A.A. name to any related facility or outside enterprise, lest problems of money, property and prestige divert us from our primary purpose.

7. Every A.A. group ought to be fully self-supporting, declining outside contributions.

8. Alcoholics Anonymous should remain forever nonprofessional, but our service centers may employ special workers.

9. A.A., as such, ought never be organized; but we may create service boards or committees directly responsible to those they serve.

10. Alcoholics Anonymous has no opinion on outside issues; hence the A.A. name ought never be drawn into public controversy.

11. Our public relations policy is based on attraction rather than promotion; we need always maintain personal anonymity at the level of press, radio, and films.

12. Anonymity is the spiritual foundation of all our traditions, ever reminding us to place principles before personalities.

of discipline, one that can be extremely consistent with the Christian faith.

Why are the Twelve Steps and the process of recovery that they produce so powerful? I will try to answer that, referring to the steps and the traditions as we go along (see figures 8 and 9).

THE TWELVE STEPS AS A SPIRITUAL PROCESS

The process of recovery is an *antidote to shame*. The main fuel of shame is the idea that, "I am a bad, worthless person. If you knew me you would hate me." In Twelve-Step meetings, people will come to know a sex addict and every sinful, repulsive behavior that he or she has ever done. When you tell your sexual addiction story during a meeting, instead of running out of the room, the other addicts will embrace you, accept you, and love you. They have done many of the same things and perhaps more. They understand what it's like to be in your shoes.

This process of "being known" is practiced in Steps One, Four, and Five. In Step One addicts admit that they are powerless and that their lives have become unmanageable. To do this, addicts are asked to describe the behaviors they did that are unmanageable. First steps are often narrative histories of how bad things got. When a person is able to do this they are finally accepting that they have a problem. Addicts say to themselves and to the group that they have tried to stop but can't. They humbly recognize that help is beyond their control and they need others to help them.

This process of humility in the first step requires a genuine sense of powerlessness. It is part of our sinful nature to think we can control our own behavior and that we don't need anyone else or God. The first step lays the groundwork for being able to realize the need to surrender to God.

Steps Four and Five describe the process of *confession*. Addicts take a moral inventory of their lives and admit their wrongs to God, themselves, and others. The Twelve-Step Program recognizes that it is one thing to admit your wrongs to yourself, but quite another thing to tell someone else. To tell someone else requires honesty and challenges the shame that the addict normally feels. Addicts also accept the risk of being rejected. A great sense of freedom results when someone else knows their secret and nothing terrible happens to them.

In the act of confession, grace is experienced. The church recognizes this. We know that God is living and forgiving, but it is one thing to know it and another to experience it. Telling your story to someone else is to experience the forgiveness of God.

Traditionally, Steps Four and Five have been told to clergy. Today, this may still be the case, but it doesn't have to be so. The fourth and fifth steps are also not a one-time experience. The tenth step invites the addict to continue to take moral inventory and when he is wrong to admit it "promptly."

The Twelve Steps are an "honesty" program. One of the main dynamics that fuels addiction along with shame is the fear of being found out. Addicts tell many lies and lead double lives. The honesty and confession of the program removes the stress of this fear. It also helps them to be honest, humble, self-aware, and always on guard against immoral and sinful behaviors.

Steps Two and Three invite addicts to *surrender their lives* to a "Higher Power." The second step recognizes that it is only a Power greater than ourselves that can restore us to sanity, and the third step tells us to turn the will and control of our life over to that Power. The program uses the term "Higher Power" to leave the interpretation of that Power to the addict. Christians practicing the second and third step will be aware that this Power is God in Jesus Christ.

Bill Wilson intentionally used the neutral language of "Higher Power" because he found that many recovering alcoholics were uncomfortable defining it as God. They were not atheists, but they had been so preached at, so judged by the church, and so ostracized that they disliked religious language and religious people. The nonthreatening language helps many addicts come to God slowly and in their own way.

Sex addicts' image of God is usually not a friendly one. If they were raised in religious or Christian homes, their experience may have been so painful and abusive that the thought of church or God is associated with that pain. If these people are to come back to the church, it must happen slowly and in their own time.

It is not simply the addiction that makes an addict's life unmanageable. Step Six acknowledges defects of character that may have led to addiction, and Step Seven humbly asks God to remove these defects. Recovering addicts are constantly searching their personality to discover these defects. What are their shortcomings, angers, resentments, fears, and anxieties? Addicts must check these out with their sponsor and their group, where they get constant feedback. Steps Six and Seven describe a process much like sanctification, where we improve our lives and become more dedicated to God.

The steps also recognize that for improvement to occur there must also be *restitution*. Steps Eight and Nine involve making a list of all people that have been harmed by past behavior. Addicts then try to make amends, unless to do so would harm someone. In these two steps addicts recognize that they are responsible for past behavior and responsible to ask for forgiveness, make restitution, and change behaviors.

Sometimes people who have been harmed are not alive, around, or available. Sometimes the damage is of a nature that can't be repaired or repaid. Sometimes to contact a person who has been harmed would violate the confidentiality of a situation or otherwise further harm that person. Nevertheless, the addict should recognize the harm, accept it, and even attempt some kind of vicarious or symbolic restitution. For example, if a sex addict can't fully repay the money spent on pornography, he or she can contribute to groups that work to eliminate pornography. And they certainly can change their behavior so as not to commit the harm again.

Accomplishing Steps Eight and Nine is often a lifetime process. Before undertaking restitution, therefore, the addict should always check with a sponsor or group to make sure the plan is a good one, the time is right, and that someone won't be harmed. Only then should they go forward with their plans, and thereby enjoy the peace of living responsibly, repaying debts, and changing destructive behaviors.

Countless recovering sex addicts whom I have talked to are actually "grateful" for their consequences, for it rescues them from the delusions they have suffered and shows them how damaging their behaviors have been. They can then realize that "my *behaviors* are bad, but *I* am not. Consequences remind me of my bad behaviors and force me to make the changes I need to be healthy. Consequences also give me the opportunity to make restitution to those I have harmed."

Consequences of sinful sexual behaviors may be very painful. Ultimately the addict must grieve deeply over harms done and relationships damaged. When I say that sex addicts may be grateful for consequences, I mean that they have embraced this pain and loss and are still thankful because their life now is better in a host of ways than it was before.

It is also important to remember that a sex addict was usually an abused child. Because of their wounds, they will naturally resist any form of punishment. Recovery teaches sex addicts that they did not deserve the abuse they received as a child, that they were not responsible for that abuse, but that they are responsible now for the consequences of current behavior.

Consequences can be a *loving* reminder of correct behaviors. Many who think that sex addicts are trying to avoid consequences would like to see them punished very severely. Consequences, however, need to be enforced fairly out of our love and hope for the restoration of a sex addict.

When the prodigal son returned home after a number of sins including sexual ones, the father celebrated and threw a party. The faithful brother was furious and confronted his father about this unfairness. Many accusers of sex addicts may be like the brother. They complain that it's unfair to restore someone to the community of faith after a great sin.

A key in this story is the *humility* of the prodigal son. He has learned through the consequences of his behavior that he is no better than his father's servants. A person who has, through his or her own sinfulness, been driven to despair and yet returns humbly and in total need of God's nurture, forgiveness, and care is a person to celebrate.

The Twelve Steps are an effective form of *spiritual discipline*. Step Eleven suggests that this spirituality is an ongoing process of conscious contact with God. Addicts are left to define their own program for how conscious contact takes place. It may be prayer, meditation, or attending church. The Twelve-Step fellowships don't attempt to define this process any further because to do so would create a religion in itself. Step Eleven recognizes that spiritual discipline is essential if an addict is to stay sober.

Step Eleven also recognizes that the individual will of addicts has almost destroyed their lives. It encourages them to surrender that will to God and to discover God's will for them. By prayerfully seeking God's will, they enjoy his peace and serenity.

The final step in this program recognizes that addicts have had a spiritual awakening and that they must tell others about this. Is not this the story of evangelism? Christians, too, learn to share what Christ has done to straighten out their lives. By witnessing, addicts and Christians relive the power of their transformation. Personal evangelism is a key to both the church and to the Twelve-Step program.

The Twelve Steps are effective because they are not to be practiced in isolation, but in *fellowship*. The program recognizes that addicts have struggled for years in silence, leading a double life, trying to work things out for themselves. The Twelve-Step programs surround the addict with fellowship. Addicts enjoy the strength that numbers bring, and the grace of meeting with people who have done the same behaviors and who hear about theirs without judgment. They benefit from the wisdom of older members who have achieved ongoing sobriety. They receive support, encouragement, and affirmation as they work on their program. And they learn accountability as they begin to answer to a group.

Another strength of the Twelve Steps is that it strongly suggests that an addict have a sponsor, usually a person who has been practicing the steps for a longer time and whose sobriety is very stable. The sponsor spends time with the sponsoree outside of meetings to discuss the steps and the progress of the individual's program. They may talk on the phone "any time, day or night," particularly if the addict is in danger of recommitting the addictive behavior.

This personal relationship is powerful because the addict has probably come from a dysfunctional family, and the sponsor relationship begins to repair the wounds of that dysfunction. It teaches the addict that at least one person can be trusted and counted on for love and support. However, the sponsor is not always accepting, but rather would confront the addict whenever he or she seems on the verge of relapse.

A sponsor is like a spiritual leader or discipler. For example, Paul was Timothy's discipler and spiritual sponsor. Paul's letters to Timothy are full of spiritual encouragement, advice, teaching, and even admonishment.

A final reason the Twelve Steps are effective is that they are concrete. They are tangible. They are a *formula* to follow. Addicts look for black and white solutions to problems, and the Twelve Steps are a list, a direction, a recipe of recovery. Addicts can sink their teeth into the steps and do something.

In summary, the Twelve Steps are a recovery tool. In many ways, they follow a Christian pattern for recovery: Step One recognizes one's *sin* and the futility of one's effort to control it; Steps Two and Three call on God for *salvation*; Steps Four, Five, and Ten call for *confession*; Steps Six and Seven encourage *sanctification*; Steps Eight and Nine require making amends and *restitution*; Step Eleven demands *spiritual discipline*; and Step Twelve encourages *evangelism*. Christians can use these Twelve Steps as a means of disciplining themselves spiritually.

Imagine going to a typical church service on Sunday and telling the exact nature of your sexual sins. What would the response of the pastor and congregation be? It is easy to see why many who have been estranged from a judgmental church find great spiritual strength in the Twelve-Step Program.

One Christian friend told me that most churches he knows are like new car showrooms. We shine ourselves up and go there in order to sell ourselves as being wonderful. A Twelve-Step meeting, however, is like a car body shop. People go there because they are bumped and bruised and need help.

I know a sex addict who masturbated, used pornography, visited prostitutes, and had numerous affairs. He had been to the best therapists and doctors money could buy. A Christian, he had also consulted with pastors and read the Bible and numerous books of theology. Nothing seemed to help. Because he was a proud man and a professional, he really thought that he should be able to help himself, so he never told anyone his secret.

One day a friend confronted him and said he knew about some of the sexual behaviors. A recovering alcoholic, this friend said the behaviors reminded him of his own drinking days and told the addict how his life had been changed by practicing the steps. Tired of maintaining his veil of secrecy and impressed by the humility and gentle nature of his friend, the sex addict decided to seek out help.

Together, they located a Sex Addicts Anonymous meeting. The sex addict attended a meeting, and he was amazed that he was not the only one struggling with this problem. Soon he started down the Twelve-Step road to recovery, admitting his failures and making restitution where he could.

The sex addict's life began to improve. Although he still had to suffer the painful consequences of his abusive behavior, he found a new sense of peace and happiness and felt closer to God than he'd ever felt before. By practicing the Twelve Steps, he began to heal from his sexual addiction.

10.

Confronting the Sexual Addict

If you suspect someone of being a sexual addict, you must get them help before they further destroy themselves and others. To ignore this behavior would be to become a party to their sin. This process of confronting an addict with his or her behavior is called *intervention*.

In Matthew 18:15–17, Jesus outlines a four-part approach for confronting a sinner. First, you talk to the sinner alone. If he listens, you have gained a brother, and he need not be publicly humiliated. Second, if he doesn't listen, you should go to him with one or two others who will confirm what you are saying. Third, if he *still* doesn't listen, then you need to involve the church. Finally, if he doesn't respond to the discipline of the church, he should be shunned.

ONE-TO-ONE INTERVENTION

If you are thinking of confronting a sexual addict alone, you will first need to take stock of yourself. First, are you able to confront the addict with a spirit of love and gentleness? If you are angry, judgmental, or feeling punitive, you should let someone else be involved in the intervention. The main criterion for any intervention is that you do it out of love, not out of judgment.

Second, are you in a codependent relationship with the

addict? If you desperately need a sex addict's approval, you will not have the strength or the objectivity to confront him on your own.

Third, is your own conscience clear in this area of your life? Most sex addicts can tell you about people who were angry with them about their sexual behaviors who had committed those same behaviors.

Finally, will you be able to follow through on the intervention? Personal intervention will include setting down ultimatums and following through. You should never attempt this kind of intervention if you are not strong enough personally to do what you say you're going to do.

Once you have answered these questions and decided to go ahead with the intervention, you should tell someone else about your plan. Telling someone will give you the strength and courage to do it, and will also help you to check your motivations.

If there are no roadblocks and your motivation is good, you should then courageously confront the behaviors that you know about. You might begin by saying, "I care about you, but I am concerned about some of your behaviors. By those I mean . . . (list the facts of the sexual acting out that are known)."

You should also share your own weaknesses and experience with getting help, "I know what it's like to do these things. These are some of the addictive behaviors that I have done . . . (describe what they were). I was out of control. But I was afraid that if people knew what I was doing, they would hate me. Finally, I found help . . . (describe your personal process of getting help)." If you can't relate personally to the sexual or addictive behaviors, you might describe someone you know about (without mentioning names) who had similar problems and got help.

Try to empathize with the sex addict: "It must be really lonely. You must be tired and frightened." Avoid diagnosing the problem; don't say: "You must be really angry" or "You must come from a really screwed-up family." Also avoid judgmental comments: "How could you do such things? Didn't you know any better?"

Carefully distinguish between the effect the sex addict's behavior has had on you from the effect it's had on others. "When you did (again list a behavior), it really hurt me and I got really angry" or "That really embarrassed me or caused me harm" (describe the exact nature of the harm). Do not list harms to others, at least not at this time. This would only serve to make the sex addict defensive. If a sex addict does become defensive at this point, you might say, "I'm not trying to judge you, and right now I don't need you to defend your behaviors. I need you to listen to what I'm saying. I just want you to know how you affected me."

Next you would state how you would like the sex addict's behavior to change around you. For example, "Please do not tell those sexual jokes around me anymore. Please do not ask me for sex. Please don't touch me in that way. Please don't ask me for (describe certain sexual behaviors). I expect you to be sexually faithful to me." Then you can describe the consequences to the sex addict if he or she is not able to observe the stated boundaries. "If you do these things again, this is what I will do" (describe the *exact* nature of what you will do).

For a spouse, for example, this could be, "If you continue these sexual behaviors, you need to know that I won't be able to live under the same roof with you. I can't stand to see you destroying yourself, our marriage, and our family." An employer might state obvious vocational consequences. A pastor would state consequences in terms of church membership.

The final component of one-to-one intervention is to state clearly where help is available and how to get it. You should have phone numbers ready for counselors, treatment centers, and Twelve-Step fellowships. You may offer to drive the person to a counselor, or you may even offer to help pay for therapeutic help.

After all of this, you should restate your love and concern for the addict. "I care for you. I value our relationship and want to see it continue. I hope and pray that you can get some help for yourself." State your faith in a personal God who loves and cares for the sex addict, and offer Scripture that underlines God's love and acceptance for the repentant sinner.

A sex addict might be very defensive about religion, but you should not argue or get defensive in return. To do so would be the quickest way to end the conversation. Instead, say something like, "It must be really hard to have prayed and not get the answer you want. I sometimes believe that God works in quiet ways, less dramatic than we might expect. Sometimes I don't understand how he works. All I know right now is that I'm willing to help you" (again list the ways that you are willing to help).

The worst case scenario is that the sex addict won't listen to you, won't accept help, or will even become angry with you. If this happens, don't let it get you down. The anger or defensiveness has nothing to do with what you have done, how you have done it, or you as a person. Sex addiction is a powerful disease. A sex addict's reaction is a symptom of how tightly the disease still controls him or her.

GROUP INTERVENTION

If the sex addict listens, then he or she may be open to getting some help. If he or she doesn't listen, you should take one or two others, as Jesus instructs, to support you and to provide more evidence. Sex addicts who are denying that they have a problem need to see evidence—direct statements of the proof. They might also need to be convinced that not just one person sees the sinful behavior. Sex addicts are very skilled at deceiving others and at talking their way out of accusations, which is easier to do one on one.

Dr. Richard Irons of Golden Valley Health Center says that individually confronting addicts is like playing one-on-one basketball against Michael Jordan. We won't win. They are too skilled at denial and delusion. He said, however, that when we take a team of people, even if none of them are NBA caliber, the team will probably get the job done.

The elements of two or more people confronting the sexual addict are identical to the individual intervention. Every person in the room would simply take turns stating care and concern, providing evidence, defining boundaries, laying down consequences, and offering help.

CHURCH INTERVENTION

Jesus tells us that if group intervention fails, then we should involve the church—assuming, of course, that the sex addict is a member of a church. At this point a pastor, elders, or other members of the church will visit the addict in order to state the truth and the "bottom line" very clearly. If the sex addict is a pastor, church members can and should confront him or her.

If the pastor has engaged in exploitive or abusive behavior, higher level church officials must be involved in intervention. The local and the national church have a legal stake in seeing that the right thing is done, for churches have been sued because they didn't take direct and immediate action. If the church has knowledge of sexual misconduct and doesn't act on it, any future person with whom this pastor might be sexual would be entitled to sue for gross negligence.

INVOLVING THE FAMILY

There is a broader question that Jesus doesn't directly address in this passage: How much should family members be involved in an intervention? I think that they must be. In the classic alcoholic intervention, family members, friends, employers, church members, and any other concerned people who have knowledge of the facts can be involved in a group intervention. This should be led by a counselor or pastor experienced in the art of doing an intervention. The role of this moderator is *extremely* important. The moderator orchestrates the intervention in the style that will be the most likely to get the sex addict some help.

Often a moderator will want to gather the group together before the intervention. In this meeting the moderator should obtain facts, understand each person's boundaries, fully account for consequences that might take place if the addict is not willing to get help, and make a complete list of where help is available and who is willing to assist the addict in getting that help. The moderator might rehearse with people what they will say and how and when they will say it.

The moderator will decide if any person intending to participate has the maturity or emotional objectivity to do so. For example, a family member might be learning about certain of the sex addict's sexual behaviors for the first time, and her own level of hurt and anger might be such that she could not participate without getting emotionally out of control. This would only cause the sex addict to be defensive or distracted from the important business of the intervention.

During the intervention the moderator leads the entire meeting, calling on people to say what they need to say at appropriate times. He or she might start, "We are here because we love you and are very concerned about you. We are not here to judge you, but we do need to talk with you about certain of your behaviors that concern us very deeply." From this point the style is very consistent with the elements of intervention already described. Participants might want to state their concern, their knowledge of the facts, the effect the sexual behaviors have had on them personally, their boundaries, and consequences that they will enforce if help is not sought and behaviors changed.

Finally, as Jesus says, if the sex addict resists all these steps, those involved must not associate with him. A spouse should take steps to separate himself or herself from the addict, friends should refuse to socialize with the addict, and the church should bar the addict from participating in the Lord's Supper. Shunning a person is intensely painful for everyone, but it is the most caring thing to do, and the most honest. The sexual behaviors involved, whatever they are, are intolerable and must stop. Only by facing the consequences of their behavior will some addicts be shaken into acknowledgment of their problem.

Everyone concerned must discipline themselves to enforce the consequences, for if you let the sex addict get away with her behavior, she will believe that she has manipulated the system again and that she can repeat the behaviors without suffering the consequences.

Occasionally, family members deny the behavior as vehemently as the sex addicts themselves. As I have said, the family, and certainly the spouse, are often the last people to accept the reality of inappropriate sexual behaviors. However, even if the sex addict has been very good at deceiving them, at some gut level they will know what is going on, and finding out the truth will "make sense" to them. Group interventions in these cases will involve those who do accept the truth and are willing to take action. Family members who have not accepted the problem should not be present at the intervention. They should, however, be kept informed about the plan of action.

In some situations family members in a sex addict's family may be as sick as he is. Anyone planning interventions of any kind should be aware that they will need to deal with more than one individual; in fact, they will need resources for the whole family. Helping the family will be just as important as helping the sexual addict.

Besides being aware of family dynamics, the moderator must consider the possible system-wide dynamics and be ready to intervene with them as well. This may seem like an overwhelming task, for some of the systems are large and the individual problems can seem endless. In these situations, you should never try to be the Lone Ranger. We will need allies.

Interventions are highly emotional. There may be anger, denial, delusions, and high drama. Sex addicts may deny the behavior entirely, or play the role of victim. Sometimes a sexual addict will use religious forms of denial to avoid getting help. In a recent intervention that I witnessed, a group of church leaders and their pastor intervened with a member who had had a number of affairs with women in the church. The man became intensely emotional, crying and asking for God's forgiveness. His behavior, however, didn't change. This same group intervened again. Again, the man cried for forgiveness. However, this time the group asked him to leave the church until he could demonstrate ongoing sexual sobriety. This man became furious and accused the group of not practicing God's love and forgiveness. In a short time he managed to create divisions in the church—all in the name of God's love and forgiveness.

Those who intervene must put on the "whole armor of God" to fight the wiles of the devil. But be of good courage. God is with you. Do what you need to do in love, and God will guide the process.

11.

Treatment for Sexual Addiction

Once someone has agreed to get treatment for sexual addiction, the first step is to find someone who can determine whether he or she really is a sex addict. There are a growing number of counselors who are trained to do this. They will ask for a history of behaviors and feelings and give their opinion about what direction treatment should take.

Hospitals such as Golden Valley Health Center are able to interview people and give an opinion about what treatment is needed as well as recommend places where it is available. Written diagnostic tests are also available. The oldest and the most widely validated are instruments that Patrick Carnes has designed, the Sexual Addiction Screening Test (SAST) and the Sexual Addiction Inventory (SAI). The SAST is very short and the SAI is very long.

Once a diagnosis of sexual addiction has been made, five basic components of treatment based on the sexual addiction cycle are vital to recovery from sexual addiction (see figure 10): stopping the sexual behaviors, stopping the rituals, stopping the fantasizing, healing the despair, and healing from shame.

STOPPING THE SEXUAL BEHAVIORS

The first step a sexual addict will have to take is stopping the sexual behaviors, both the building-block behaviors of masturbation, fantasy, and use of pornography, and the other behaviors they

146

may have done but don't do regularly. Just as alcoholics need to stop drinking before they can be treated, so do sex addicts need to stop acting out before they can deal with other issues in the recovery process.

I feel it is vitally important for sex addicts to stop all sexual behaviors for at least ninety days. They should agree to a total abstinence or "celibacy" contract, which states that they will not be sexual with themselves (through masturbation) or anyone else. This contract reverses a sex addict's core belief and shows him or her that "Sex is *not* my most important need."

Abstinence can't continue forever if the sex addict is married. In this regard recovering from sexual addiction is not like recovering from alcoholism. Alcoholics can abstain from alcohol for the rest of their lives, but sex addicts will not usually abstain from sex. Recovering from sexual addiction is more analogous to recovering from food addiction. Food addicts can't stop eating forever, but they can learn to eat when their body is hungry to nourish themselves. Married sex addicts, likewise, will learn that sex with their spouse is appropriate and beautiful when, instead of being a way to avoid intimacy or escape negative feelings, it expresses the intimacy of the marriage.

Once an addict has determined to stop his or her behavior, he or she then needs to find a setting in which this abstinence can best be achieved. Some sex addicts can achieve sobriety simply by going to Twelve-Step groups. Sometimes going to meetings will be combined with counseling. Counseling in itself is usually inadequate; I know only one or two sex addicts who have achieved abstinence through counseling alone.

If Twelve-Step meetings and counseling are not enough to stop sexual behaviors, the next step should be an outpatient treatment program, similar to outpatient programs for alcoholism. The programs provide three to four hours of treatment per day, three to four days a week. The addict is usually allowed to live at home and maintain employment. Outpatient programs provide therapy, Twelve-Step support, and education. In most of them families are involved as well.

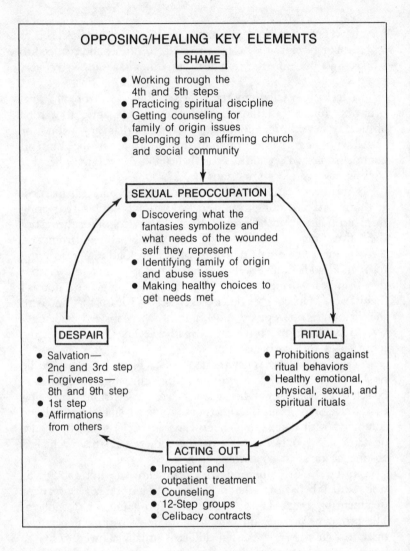

Figure 10: The Recovery Cycle

In some cases more aggressive inpatient treatment is needed. This means a hospital-based unit in which the addict stays in treatment full time. These programs can vary in length from two to five weeks. One week may be devoted to having immediate family members present who are invited by the addict and choose to attend.

Hospital programs are important in cases where sexual addicts experience severe depression, a major problem for many sex addicts. Some have come to the point of thinking about or trying suicide. For their own safety, around-the-clock care is important. Inpatient programs are usually supervised by medical doctors and provide twenty-four hour nursing care. Competent therapists, counselors, or psychiatrists provide counseling.

Each of these treatment levels represents tighter control over the sex addict's environment in order to support and supervise him or her. Twelve-Step groups are quick to hand out phone lists of members who can be called if there is a temptation to act out. Outpatient programs provide this as well, plus they offer more intense therapy and education. Inpatient programs offer twenty-four hour monitoring and supervision. Some addicts in the first days desperately need this in order to break the cycle of addiction.

Having to go to an inpatient program should not be interpreted as a sign of failure or moral weakness, only as a sign of the strength of the disease and the level to which it has progressed. There are no programs that I am aware of where addicts are locked up and watched every minute. Ultimately, even in inpatient programs, sex addicts must learn to monitor themselves.

STOPPING THE RITUALS

In the early days of recovery, sex addicts usually have no idea that they go through rituals before sexually acting out, and helping them to recognize the rituals is usually a simple matter of telling them what rituals are. In a Twelve-Step program addicts will learn about themselves by hearing about the behavior and rituals of others. While everyone's rituals are different, there are common elements, deceptions, delusions, and strategies.

Many times the shorter rituals are easy to discover and to understand, but the longer ones are more difficult. Sex addicts who get triggered by some stimulus on TV, get into their cars, obtain money at the instant teller machine, and go to a massage parlor, pursue a short ritual. Other sex addicts who flirt with potential partners, engage them in friendship over the course of weeks, months, or even years, and eventually act out sexually with them pursue a longer ritual.

One of the keys to stopping sexual acting out will be to stop the ritual. If alcoholics allow themselves to go into a bar, they will probably take a drink. The same is true for sex addicts. When the process of the ritual begins, acting out will be the result.

For example, if acting out includes masturbating to X-rated videos, the sex addict should never rent or buy those videos, and perhaps should never enter video stores. If the addict has had an endless string of affairs and recognizes that a main part of the ritual is having lunch alone with potential partners, in the future such lunches cannot be allowed. These two examples are relatively obvious. Sex addicts have to evaluate for themselves, based on their knowledge of their ritual, what prohibitions to take.

For pastors, their whole pastoral role may be part of the ritual. They may not be aware of this, but the power, authority, and spirituality that they represent attracts others to them. The way they teach, preach, counsel, and care for others may all be part of the rituals which must be given up, at least for a time.

In recovery the actions that must be taken to stop rituals, the barriers that must be erected, the prohibitions that must be maintained, are called *healthy boundaries*. Sex addicts in recovery must *learn* what these have to be. In the early days they may need to be more strict than in later years, but the principle is, "I must go to any length to recover." The Twelve-Step groups, sponsors, counselors, and treatment centers will know how to *educate* sex addicts about their rituals. Addicts will be encouraged to make lists of what they are. Then they will be encouraged to make other lists of healthy boundaries that they will maintain.

The book of Hebrews says, "My son, do not make light of the Lord's discipline" (Heb. 12:5). Discipline has both the negative aspect of punishment and the positive aspect of learning healthy behaviors. Healthy discipline, or positive boundaries, can be emotional, physical, sexual, and certainly spiritual in nature.

Healthy emotional discipline will result in addicts feeling better about themselves. They should beware, however, of all those people or books that tell them to start liking themselves. For sex addicts who are abuse victims it is never that easy.

The key is discipline, starting with what the recovery community calls "self-talk," messages that addicts daily remind themselves. Sex addicts might make a list of the good things in their life. At first, they might not believe these affirmations. Belief will come after the discipline of practice. One of the old A.A. slogans says, "Fake it till you make it."

Sex addicts should make a point of associating with people who affirm them. They should make a list of people who help them feel good about themselves, and a second list of people to avoid— those who make them feel ashamed. They need to tell themselves, "I deserve to be with loving and affirming people. I can avoid people, including family members, who only tell me shaming messages."

Physical discipline is easier to understand than emotional discipline. Sex addicts may not have taken care of themselves for years. They must learn, for example, to eat nutritious foods, get enough sleep, exercise regularly, or stop smoking. It is always amazing to find out how much better they will feel emotionally and spiritually if they do some of these things. When they are not used to doing them, they must practice, starting slowly, and progressing.

For married sexual addicts in recovery, positive sexual discipline will mean practicing healthy sexual behaviors with a spouse. My friends Joyce and Clifford Penner have written several helpful books on this subject.[1]

In addition, anything done to nourish yourself in positive physical ways is also having a healthy sexual relationship with yourself. Think of simple things like buying nice sheets for your bed, taking a bubble bath, exercising regularly, or getting a manicure. A healthy sexual relationship in a marriage depends on mutual respect of each other's body and on doing nice things for each other. Those who don't have a partner will nevertheless respect their own body and do nice things for it.

Spiritual discipline may come for sex addicts, at least at first, in quiet meditation, allowing the "still, small voice" of God to speak. Sex addicts have tried to be in control for years. It is now time for them to be quiet, to listen for the voice of God (which probably won't be as dramatic as they would like), and to allow God to be in control.

Spiritual discipline also includes finding a church where they will feel comfortable. The pastor should be willing to hear and accept their story, and they should be a part of a small group, such as a Twelve-Step group, that will give them encouragement and support.

Several Twelve-Step fellowships are Christian in their orientation. Overcomers Outreach has developed 750 Twelve-Step groups in churches around the country. Call them and find out if there is a group in your area.

Finally, sex addicts will come to prayer, Bible study, and meditation gradually, out of quietness, humility, and support. The Catholic tradition is historically more successful than many Protestant ones in providing people with spiritual directors who will guide the spiritual life and provide positive role modeling. This tradition is also very good at encouraging people to go on individual and group spiritual retreats. Many other churches are embracing these principles of "discipleship." A sex addict will need this kind of support and guidance. Just as a sex addict needs a sponsor in the Twelve-Step program, he or she will also need one in the Christian journey.

Positive discipline establishes new, positive rituals for the sex addict. If sex addicts bring the energy to these new rituals that they devoted to the old ones, they will be extremely successful.

STOPPING FANTASY

Stopping fantasy is perhaps one of the hardest aspects of recovery. Addicts can simply think about their behaviors for stimulation, and a sex addict has countless memories and fantasies to recall at a wink of an eye. Sights, sounds, words, and people can instantly trigger a fantasy. Trying to stop is extremely frustrating because these images can't be erased.

Psychologists advocate several approaches for stopping fantasy. The most basic is to try to stop the fantasies. When fantasies occur, addicts are encouraged to remember that fantasy is a drug for them and to stop fantasizing. They may be told to switch to something else in their mind. As any sex addict will tell you, however, this approach doesn't work too well. They have played too many mind games, held on to too many delusions, and had too many stimuli locked away in their memories.

Another strategy is to do something negative when fantasies occur. This is called behavioral conditioning. The principle is to begin associating pain or punishment with the sexual fantasy. For example, if addicts are fantasizing about an affair, they are reminded to think of the worst possible outcome of that affair. I talked to one patient who wore a rubber band around his wrist. Whenever he fantasized he snapped his wrist with that rubber band. He hoped to create the association of pain with his fantasies.

The problem with this strategy is that it allows sex to remain or to become a completely negative experience. If addicts condition themselves to associate sex with pain, at what point do they allow themselves to experience healthy and positive sexuality?

I believe that fantasy is a symptom of the emotional and spiritual condition of sexual addicts. When they are lonely, tired, angry, sad, anxious, or afraid, their fantasies take over their thinking. Fantasizing is their way of distracting themselves from painful feelings. If they simply try to stop fantasizing, they will not learn to understand those feelings.

Usually feelings stem from a painful childhood or recent memories. Sex addicts are afraid to examine their feelings because they are usually painful. The sex addict has learned to avoid pain, and it will take courage and practice for them to start dealing with it. However, if sex addicts begin to understand and allow themselves to feel, they have begun the battle.

In recovery, addicts must be taught that they have choices about dealing with feelings. When they are tired and lonely and beginning to fantasize, they should ask themselves, "What does this fantasy mean? What am I feeling? Am I sad, lonely, afraid, or what?" They can call someone to talk to. They can go to a meeting. The key is learning to *tell* someone what the feelings are and getting support from them.

Talking about stopping fantasy, rituals, and acting out can be extremely threatening to sex addicts, for these behaviors have helped them survive. Perhaps the addict was abandoned as a three-year-old. Frightened and alone, she turned to a behavior that calmed her and allowed her to escape, at least in her mind. Would she not cling to that behavior? Only in later life does she learn that this behavior will also kill her. Somehow, this doesn't make sense. How could something so helpful be so deadly? This confusion is a barrier to giving up addictive behavior.

Sex addicts are adults who know that their behavior is dangerous. Yet inside them is a child who knows that giving up that behavior will cause great pain. Addicts' lives are a tug-of-war between the adult and the child. Before addicts can find healing and become fully adult, they must confront the fears of the child within.

HEALING DESPAIR

Sexual addicts experience deep emotional and spiritual despair. They believe that there is no hope, that life will never get better, that if there is a God, he doesn't care. Many despairing addicts think of suicide.

Although despair seems to be a negative emotion, it can lead to greater good. For despair is not the result of God abandoning the sexual addict. Rather, *despair results when addicts try to help themselves*. Despair forces addicts to find out that they can't heal themselves, that their efforts are never good enough, that they need other people, and that they need God. Seen in this way the feeling of despair can lead to surrender to God. Christians, therefore, should not be quick to heal the sense of despair through easy solutions.

Sexual addicts will recover from despair gradually, as they recover from their addictive behavior. They will be encouraged by the testimonies of recovering addicts in Twelve-Step programs, where they will learn that people can change and things do get better. They will gain self-confidence as they learn to control their behavior, rituals, and fantasies. They will gain strength and hope by admitting their addiction and by testifying to their recovery. This gradual process of self-affirmation will stop the feeling of despair and also begin to heal the sense of shame.

HEALING SHAME

Like despair, shame is not all bad. Shame points us to our own unworthiness and our need for God. An abuse victim, however, has assumed an *identity* of shame and feels completely worthless.

To deal with unhealthy shame, sexual addicts must delve into their family background. While both individual and group therapy can be effective ways of exploring past abuse, I strongly recommend group therapy as opposed to or in addition to individual counseling. For one thing, many addicts learn about their own abuse by seeing other addicts deal with theirs. They may have repressed their abuse memories because they are so painful that the mind refuses to remember them. Seeing others accept and deal with their abuse helps addicts feel safe enough to let the memories back into the conscious mind.

Painful memories will come back as the addict is ready to deal with them. I believe God is in control of this process and does not give the addict more to cope with than he or she is prepared to handle.

It usually takes about two years for a sexual addict to recall and deal with memories of abuse. If the abuse is more severe the time will be longer. It is not uncommon for certain memories of abuse to surface right away and for others to take longer. At a reunion of our sexual dependency unit, one female addict who had been released eighteen months before suddenly remembered incest with her father. Because she was back in a community where she felt safe, her mind allowed her to remember this extremely important abuse.

Sexual addicts may be discouraged that this process takes so long and is so painful. However, the *intensity* of the experience will diminish over time and periods of joy and peace will increase. As they recover from their addiction, tell others what they have done, learn to share who they really are, and make amends, they will find healing from their sense of shame.

Only God can ultimately heal the sense of shame. Christ died not only to take away our sins, but also to vanquish our shame. Through him we will find freedom from shame, despair, and addiction.

OTHER ADDICTIONS

Many sex addicts suffer from other addictions, such as to alcohol or drugs. When sexual addiction is in check and recovery has started, other addictions can gain strength. Addicts will always be tempted to escape their painful feelings, and if one "drug"— sex—is taken away, others can step in. Sex addicts must be aware that this can happen and be prepared to bring the same recovery principles they learned about sex to other problems.

THE PROCESS OF RECOVERY

Sexual addiction is a lifelong disease. The treatment strategies described above elaborate the healing that needs to take place in the first several years of recovery. This period of time will be the most intense. Sex addicts will always need to go to meetings, get counseling, have a sponsor, and maintain their spiritual discipline. When they do these things they will continue to grow in all areas of their lives.

In summary, the following issues need to be dealt with in the recovery process: understanding abuse, healing relationships, codependency, slips and relapse, and deepening spirituality.

UNDERSTANDING ABUSE

As I mentioned earlier, sexual addicts will need to deal with the abuse they suffered in the past. They may or may not be able to get in touch with the abuse they experienced, depending on how young they were at the time and how violent it was. Many alumni of Golden Valley say they were abused before the age of two or three. They have difficulty remembering these times. Sometimes violent abuse gets repressed and will take longer to remember.

Group therapy provides a safe environment in which sex addicts may remember what needs to be remembered. In groups, others dealing with their abuse may help addicts get in touch with what happened to them. At other times education about abuse will be enough to trigger memories.

Sex addicts will not want to accept their abuse, even the most obvious and violent kinds, because of shame. A part of them believes that they are responsible for the abuse and even deserved it. They will need direct, assertive, and continuing support to counteract that belief.

The addict's high pain threshold will make them want to minimize the effects of the abuse. They will want to forgive and forget, to move on, to think only about the future. However, they will need to be gently reminded that strength comes, not by denying their feelings, but by allowing the feelings to enter.

Recovering sex addicts must learn to grieve. They must mourn the fact that the love they needed as a child can *never* be replaced. The pain of this realization can be overwhelming, and the addict will need support to help them experience and understand these feelings.

Sexual abuse victims will also need to express their anger. This can be done in therapy in a variety of ways. Sometimes they will need to actually confront their abuser.

There is much controversy as to whether abusers should be confronted. Some say that the act of confrontation is symbolic of accepting the abuse as powerful and of taking back control over it. When addicts confront abuse they also establish the fact that the abuser no longer has power to hurt them. On the negative side, such confrontation can be unnecessarily hurtful, particularly if the abuser doesn't have resources to deal with the hurt.

If an abuser is to be confronted, it should be done in the presence of a therapist, pastor, or counselor. This "mediator" can assure that the process is constructive. Even though the addict will express anger, he can do so in a nonjudgmental way by stating that he is doing this to heal himself and to prevent the abuser from hurting others. The addict may even say that he is confronting the abuser in order to heal their relationship.

Addicts will not heal if they don't come to a stage of forgiveness. While addicts should not be too quick to forgive and should fully experience their grief and anger, they will eventually need to move from anger to acceptance. Forgiveness becomes possible after anger and confrontation, when addicts realize that their abusers may also have been abused. One addict said, "It is easy to see why my father did what he did to me. I know my grandfather! My dad did to me what was done to him."

HEALING RELATIONSHIPS

Sex addicts must heal all of the relationships that remain important to them. This will take time but does begin to occur over the first months and years of recovery.

Key to the process is *honesty*. For years sexual addicts have been dishonest, deceiving others. The first thing to change in recovery is to be honest and no longer lie about their behavior. Next, they must stop blaming others for their problems. When addicts do this they will be able to ask what harm they have done to others and will be able to ask for forgiveness and make amends.

Next, sexual addicts must stop trying to please others at all cost. Instead of manipulating people to get their needs met, addicts must learn to ask for what they need. And they must look for supportive friends to help supply those needs. They should select friends carefully for their trustworthiness, their ability to give constructive and caring advice, and their willingness to confront old behaviors if they should happen. They must also be "safe" friends— friends who are not potential sexual partners. For this reason heterosexuals may choose to have friendships with only people of their same sex.

To establish healthy relationships, the sex addict will have to establish healthy boundaries. For example, the sex addict might say, "I will be honest with you and try not to hurt you. If I ever do anything that causes you harm, please let me know. I never intend to be sexual with you. Sometimes I don't realize my old behaviors. Please let me know if I do something that is inappropriate as you see it."

Finally, recovering sex addicts must learn how to *play*. They generally have forgotten how to play, perhaps because of their abuse. They may be workaholics, or have a hard time playing because it is a "waste of time." Playing may remind them of their abusive childhood. Yet playing is a vital element of healthy relationships. Recovery is not all pain and blackness. It is also about enjoying life and the world God has given.

CODEPENDENCY

When sex addicts have achieved a certain level of sobriety— anytime between the sixth and ninth month—the pain of loneliness and the fear of losing friends and family will hit them.

The anxiety of codependency can be frightening. Sex addicts who are married, for example, will be afraid that their spouse will leave them. In the initial recovery period, spouses may be supportive, but when they sense that the sex addict is safely recovering, they may allow their own feelings to surface. This experience will intensify the sex addict's fear.

Sex addicts will also be afraid of losing others as their behaviors become known. These can include their children, friends, other family members, church people, and co-workers. Recovering sex addicts battle the fear that if people really knew them, they would leave. During this time they will need the extra support of faithful friends.

SLIPS AND RELAPSE

The major question in recovery is whether a sexual addict can be completely healed. In recovery, a *slip* is when a sexual addict acts out once, while a *relapse* is a series of acting-out behaviors.

Remember that recovery from sexual addiction is not entirely like recovery from alcoholism. Married sex addicts can't stop all sexual behavior. Fantasy, also, is very hard to stop, especially with so many sexual stimuli in our culture. Because God created us to be sexual beings, we cannot completely deny our sexuality.

Nevertheless, we can say that recovery from sexual addiction is possible. There are countless numbers of sex addicts who enjoy years of sobriety. Golden Valley Health Center has studied a large group of alumni who have completed a five-week inpatient program, and has found dramatic reductions in the number of inappropriate sexual behaviors. This does not mean, of course, that recovery occurs smoothly. Some sex addicts will have to go to treatment more than once and will have failures along the way.

Slips and relapse are more likely to happen six to twelve months after recovery starts. During this time there are four basic dangers. First, there is *complacency*. When a certain amount of sobriety is achieved, addicts start to think that they can relax, that they have the problem "licked." When this feeling takes hold addicts may stop going to meetings, relax boundaries, and not practice other recovery strategies.

Second, as addicts recover, they will begin to experience more painful feelings because they are no longer "drugged" by their addiction. These feelings are extremely threatening to most addicts, and they will be tempted to turn to their sexual behaviors to find relief.

Third, sex addicts will start to get tired of being labeled an addict. They will grow tired of the tight boundaries. They will want to be "normal," and therefore they will lower their boundaries.

Finally, they will have to face difficult consequences, such as monetary struggles or loss of employment. They will be discouraged that their recovery is not preventing or solving these problems. This sense of futility can bring with it the temptation to act out again.

When an addict makes a slip, she should take stock of herself before she goes into relapse. A slip means that something in the recovery process has gone wrong. She may have let her boundaries become too loose, or neglect meeting with her sponsor. Or it may mean that she is avoiding a painful emotion. With the help of others, the addict should pinpoint what went wrong and avoid that mistake in the future.

When they make a slip or even when they go into relapse, addicts should not "beat themselves up" too harshly, or the resulting feeling of shame will drive them back into the acting-out cycle. Rather, they should use the slip to teach them something about their recovery.

Many sex addicts with long periods of sobriety slipped up several times in the early days of their recovery. Gradually, the recovery program will be more solidly in place and addicts will learn to anticipate "slippery times and places" more readily. They will then be able to put preventive measures in place.

The process of recovery is a strange one. It will be frightening and uncomfortable to sex addicts, and they may rebel against it. But as time goes on, the serenity of the program will begin to set in. What was once unfamiliar will become second nature, and they will embrace the process as a lifesaver.

DEEPENING SPIRITUALITY

The process of recovery is a spiritual journey. I have described the elements of it in chapter 9 as I described the Twelve Steps. In the early days of recovery an addict can experience the joy of this spiritual journey, but in the days and years to come the serenity of the journey will deepen.

First, addicts must learn to surrender themselves to God. In a moment of despair and weakness, they will give up the fight to control their life and will give that control back to God. From there they will begin the process of letting God *keep* that control.

The other key part of this spiritual journey is to feel and accept God's grace. Grace first happens when sex addicts tell their story to others and are accepted. Next, they may experience the grace of forgiveness from those they offended. Grace is the spouse who forgives a sex addict, an employer who doesn't fire an employee despite addictive behavior, and letters from church members to a pastor who is in jail. The sex addict must accept the grace that God and people offer.

The next phase of the spiritual journey is the healthy choices that sex addicts must make in their life. This involves spiritual discipline and the growing confidence that they are changed persons.

Finally, as an addict grows spiritually, he will become more vulnerable. Others will know who he is, and his relationships will deepen. He will experience full communion in the church of Christ. And he will want to bring that message of recovery to others who are suffering.

Deepening spirituality and recovery from sexual addiction are intertwined. Both are a process of healing individuals and relationships. Both involve surrender to God. Both demand daily commitment and discipline. Most of all, recovery and spirituality bring hope—hope for healing, hope for peace and serenity, hope for life changes, hope for new awareness, and hope for a deeper relationship with God.

12.

Recovery for Couples

I once began a talk about recovery for couples by saying, "There is hope for couples who suffer from this disease." One of the wives there began to sob and wail uncontrollably and did not stop crying for an hour.

The pain of sexual addiction for those who are in relationship with a sex addict is undeniable. They have been betrayed, deceived, and lied to. Their vows have been violated. They have been ignored or manipulated emotionally and physically. Their spouse may have asked them to engage in sexual practices that were repulsive and abusive. They have been placed in danger of sexually transmitted diseases. They deserve to be angry.

In spite of these facts, I still say there *is* hope for these couples. I know it to be true. Marriages can be saved. Intimacy can be achieved emotionally, physically, and spiritually. Trust can be rebuilt. This does not mean that they should deny their intense feelings of anger and betrayal, but they can work through these feelings and even use them to build stronger relationships.

This chapter investigates the nature of sexually addicted couples, and the process of recovery. The phrase *sexually addicted couples* refers to couples in which at least one person is a sex addict. The term *co-addict* refers to the spouse of a sex addict. The word *couple* generally means married couples, although much of this material can be applied to couples regardless of the legal status of their relationship. In the following pages we will look at the special needs of couples in recovery from sexual addiction.

Sexually addicted couples should try to stay together.

The biblical message is clear: a married couple becomes "one flesh." However, the secular recovery community may be suspicious of this terminology because it worries about "enmeshment," a codependent phenomenon in which one person becomes so attached to another that his or her identity becomes consumed by the other person. Some members of the recovery community worry that the Christian idea of oneness means that a spouse becomes a slave to his or her partner.

It is true that a spouse's living with a sex addict might be enabling the addiction if they are not confronting the problem and demanding change. No doubt many Christian partners have enabled addictions using their faith as part of their denial mechanism. I would argue that serving and being faithful to partners means confronting them with their sinful behavior.

To stop enmeshment, the recovery community may encourage separation and even divorce. They may help individuals to achieve sobriety but do nothing about that individual's relationships. Yet a sexually addicted couple desperately needs to bring recovery to their entire relationship. If they need sponsors, meetings, and a therapist as individuals, they will also need a sponsor, meetings, and a therapist as a couple. The sponsor should be another couple whom they can talk to when they encounter couple issues. They will need to go to Twelve-Step meetings as a couple. Recovering Couples Anonymous (see the resource section) was started for just such a purpose.

All of these meetings and therapies are time consuming and perhaps expensive. Yet this kind of support is critical for the couple, particularly in the first year. The same kind of recovery that is undertaken for the individual addict must also be undertaken for the couple.

It may be courageous and mature for a partner to leave a sex addict and not be enmeshed, but it is even more courageous and mature to stay together and work on the relationship. I am not denying that a co-addict may need to leave a relationship if the sex addict doesn't change. Not to leave may be emotionally or physically dangerous. However, the problem of enmeshment or codependency *can* be addressed while two people are living together. In fact, it might be better to practice taking care of one's self while in relationship. Addicts are good at running away from difficult relationships. Sexually addicted couples, in recovery, need not make this mistake.

Sexually addicted couples need to confront their childhood abuse.

According to Pat Carnes's research, four out of every five sex addicts have been sexually abused, three out of every four have been physically abused, and almost all of them have been emotionally abused. Carnes has also found that those who are married to sex addicts have virtually the same incidence of abuse.[1]

What are we to make of this? Abuse victims seem to find each other. For example, a man who has been abandoned by his mother may search for a woman to nurture him in a motherly way. He may find a woman whose father abandoned her, and who needs to please a man in order to get the attention and nurturing she never had. The obvious problem is that no one, not even a marriage partner, can take the place of a parent. When it becomes obvious that his wife isn't going to mother him, the husband may be enraged.

For couples, these dynamics can be extremely painful and lead to more addictive behavior. For example, the spouse of an abuse victim might say something that triggers the victim of abuse to kick into "survival" mode, becoming distant, angry, or addictive. The spouse, in turn, reacts by being angry or distant. And, in a continuing downward spiral, the victim of abuse looks for further escapes from his or her spouse, creating an addictive cycle of its own (see figure 11).

In recovery, addicts realize that abuse issues belong to parents or other perpetrators, not to the spouse. If this distinction can be made, pressure is taken off of the spouse, and greater intimacy can begin.

If the abusers were one or both of the parents, the spouse must "divorce" the parent in order not to project the abuse issues onto the spouse. How do you divorce a parent? First, if the abuse has been invasive, boundaries must be set. One man who grew anxious when his parents came to visit decided to see them only outside his home. He also decided not to allow his children to visit their grandparents alone.

"Divorcing" parents is *extremely* painful work. It is not easy to confront parents with their abuse and state whatever boundaries seem safe. The parents will be hurt, and if they are not in recovery themselves, they won't understand.

If a spouse was abandoned as a child, she will have to grieve for that parent. When these emotions are worked on, the spouse who was abandoned as a child can stop trying to get parental nurture from her spouse. With the pressure to be a parent gone, her spouse can now provide the care and nurture of a marriage partner rather than a parent.

Sexually addicted couples must strive toward intimacy.

Most sexually addicted couples have intimacy disorders because they believe that "No one will like me as I am. If you knew me you would hate me and you would *leave* me." Intimacy implies vulnerability and a willingness to let at least one other person know who you really are, what you think, and what you feel. Sex addicts can't accomplish this kind of intimacy for fear of being abandoned.

Intimacy disorder is one of the hardest parts of recovery. Trust has been violated so often, so many lies have been told, and so much emotional distance has been experienced that it becomes extremely hard to break through the feelings of anger and resentment. To

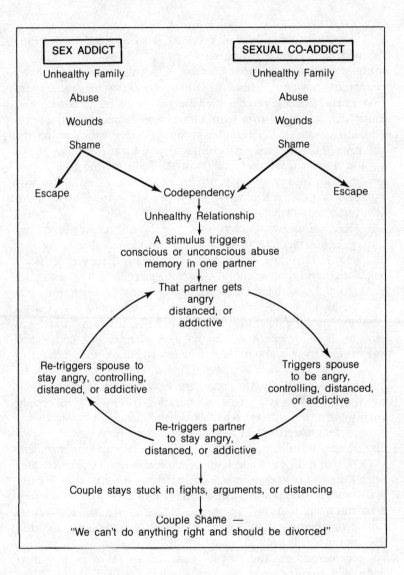

Figure 11: Couples Addiction Cycle

build intimacy, couples will need to work on communication, fighting, and playing together.

1. *Telling about past behaviors*. One hurdle to cross is to determine how much the sex addict needs to tell about past behaviors. For some there is the tendency to tell all, to blurt it out completely and get it over with. Others fear the spouse will leave if certain facts are told. This latter group will often "practice" telling the truth. They will tell a part of it and wait for the reaction. If the spouse doesn't leave then they will tell more of the truth. This process may go on for days, weeks, or months. The spouse will wonder, "When am I going to know the whole story?" and think the addict is still lying.

Recovering sex addicts may not want to deceive or lie anymore, but they are afraid of being abandoned. They may also not want to hurt their spouse by specific details. Recovery for both sex addicts and spouses means that both partners will have to take risks to tell and hear the truth. After years of deception and wondering about the truth, knowing the full story may relieve tension. Later the relief may wear off and the pain of the facts may sink in. It is important that in recovery couples give each other permission to talk about these feelings whenever they surface.

Intimacy disorder is overcome when both partners decide to take the risk to tell who they really are, how they feel, and what they are thinking. This is a *process* of practicing truth-telling. A couple may want to set time aside to talk daily. Practicing may start with insignificant material and as the couple gets more comfortable with the process of talking, more significant material can be included.

There must be some level of truth-telling. Sex addicts can't spend the rest of their lives wondering about whether their spouse will find out. Spouses can't spend the rest of their lives wondering what they will find out. The broad outline of the kinds of sexual acting out that took place should be told, but not necessarily the specifics.

Before talking, the sex addict should ask, "Why do I want to tell? What do I expect to accomplish by telling this?" When listening, the spouse of the sex addict should ask, "Why do I want to know?" Truth-telling should always take place to build intimacy, not to control feelings and behaviors or to punish. Intimacy results when truth is told for the right reasons and when it clears up all the old confusions about what was really going on.

2. *Fighting fairly.* In order for a relationship to be successful, couples need to let each other know about resentments and behaviors they don't like. Therefore I encourage them to draw up a "fighting contract" that dictates how they may fight fairly by expressing their anger in healthy ways.

First I ask couples to list their destructive fighting strategies. Such a list might include name calling, profanity, rehashing past behaviors to prove a point (sometimes called "case building"), using "you" statements, fighting in front of the children, fighting after ten P.M., using violence, and so on. The list will show them clearly where they have failed in the past.

The couple can now define the fighting contract, listing rules they *will* follow: We won't name call, use profanity, use violence, fight in front of the kids, and so on. The contract must provide *safety* so each partner feels comfortable about expressing their feelings. The contract may contain time boundaries, such as we will fight for only thirty minutes, we can take time outs, we can continue or reschedule fights, and we don't have to solve the fight today.

Couples who don't fight will still need to express their feelings, so they should set time out each week to meet together. Before they get to this "fight" they will make a list of things that made them angry or hurt that week. During the fight they simply tell their list, prefacing their list with reassuring statements like, "This list is about my feelings; it is not about wanting to get divorced" or "This list is about your behaviors and not about you" or "I need you to know that I still love you, but this list is about behaviors that I don't like." Again, the key element in all of this is safety. The rules of the contract take effect whenever there seems to be a fight starting. If they are violated, one partner will not feel safe and can get away from the fight if they need to. In recovery, these contracts must be monitored by other couples, a sponsor, a counselor, or a pastor.

3. *Playing together.* Sexually addicted couples have forgotten or never knew how to play. These couples will have to be disciplined about play, setting aside time together to do activities that they enjoy. Their play can be silly or sophisticated, ranging from building a snowman to going to an art gallery. One couple decided to decorate their yard for Christmas. The man hung lights; the woman put designs on a large wooden snowman. They transformed their front yard into a festive playland, and the neighborhood loved it.

Sexually addicted couples need to heal their sexual relationship.

The subject of building intimacy in marriage through sex deserves a book in itself. The following are highlights of areas sexually addicted couples need to examine in their sexual relationship.

Early in recovery, sex addicts will need to observe a period of celibacy in order to reverse their belief that sex is their most important need. They also need to discover that sex is not an indicator of whether their spouse loves them, and their spouses need to learn that sex is not always the way they please their partner. Abstinence takes the sexual pressure off the relationship so that the couple can work on play and communication during this time.

Throughout recovery a couple may want to be celibate in order to center themselves emotionally and spiritually. Other times for celibacy include when a spouse needs to confront his or her childhood abuse. Celibacy contracts can demand that sex happen only under certain safe conditions and in certain ways.

Sex addicts will need to lay boundaries for themselves, promising not to fantasize during sex about other partners and promising not to use sex as an escape from feelings. If the sex addict is feeling lonely, tired, angry, or afraid, this may not be a time to be sexual.

Sex addicts must learn to be sexual when it is an expression of their emotional and spiritual feelings for their partner. At first this style of sex may not be as exciting to them because it lacks adrenaline or danger, but it can be more fulfilling.

The couple may need to get some basic sexual information. There are couples in which the addict had had 500 different partners but didn't know basic sexual information. Couples should consult their doctors and counselors or read books on sexuality. I recommend the writings of Joyce and Cliff Penner.

Some sexually addicted couples experience sexual dysfunction, impotence, inhibition, or premature ejaculation. These problems may be physical; for example, impotence can be caused by diabetic complications. These problems may also be psychological. For example, incest wounds can impair a person's ability to get sexually excited. Since it is likely that both partners are sexual abuse victims, they may have a very difficult time with positive sexual expression. In these cases the couple must seek the help of a counselor who knows how to work with these problems.

The couple must learn how to express their sexual likes and dislikes. The sexual co-addict probably has never talked about what he or she likes. Doing so may involve shame or embarrassment and could take lots of patient practice.

The couple must be good at self-nurture. A healthy sexual relationship can only occur if both members of the couple like themselves as well as each other. Self-nurture involves giving oneself affirmation. It means that members of the couple take care of themselves emotionally, physically, and spiritually.

For example, one wife never wanted to have sex with her husband, the sex addict, because she felt unattractive physically. No matter how many times he told her that she was attractive to him, she wouldn't believe it, because she thought he was just lying to her in order to get her to be sexual. Until this wife likes her own body, she won't be able to share it with her husband comfortably or experience mutual enjoyment.

If the couple can work on these things they will develop a wonderful sexual intimacy. One couple told me that after their first experience of nonaddictive sex they both held each other and cried for joy. They experienced the difference between addicted sex and fulfilling sex. Instead of being in a fantasy land, for the first time they enjoyed themselves together, for who they were.

Sexually addicted couples must deal with codependency issues.

Sexually addicted couples are often two codependent people living together. The demanding partner will use the sacrificial person to get his own way. When the sacrificial person starts to stand up for her rights, the demanding partner may be threatened.

For example, one recovering sex addict had achieved about eighteen months of sobriety. His wife decided she would also get inpatient treatment for the abuse she experienced as a child. When she left for treatment, her husband, the sex addict, was tremendously anxious that she would never come back to him. He reported that this period of anxiety was as great or greater than anything he had known during the time of his sexual acting out.

The honesty that is required to have a healthy relationship is blocked by codependency. Codependency and intimacy disorder are related. Those who seek relationship and intimacy must enlist the aid of their faith. Jesus said we must be willing to lose our life in order to get it back, and the same is true of marriage. Surrendering our marriage to Christ means we are willing to live without it. This will frighten sex addicts and their spouses. But when they come to accept that God will care for them and they can survive alone, then they have the freedom to be honest about their feelings and can share personal information about who they really are.

Sexually addicted couples must overcome their shame.

Sexually addicted couples are ashamed. Not only are they ashamed individually, but they are ashamed as a couple of their codependency and intimacy disorders. Couple shame makes them feel that they have a bad marriage, and that people won't want to associate with them. One of our recovering couples moved into a new neighborhood recently. When their neighbors didn't immediately come over to introduce themselves, this couple was convinced that the whole neighborhood knew about their sexual addiction.

Couple shame makes the couple feel they are bad parents. And it tells them: "We don't have a nice house, we don't take care of our money, and we fight too much." Ultimately couple shame tells the couple that the only solution to this terrible marriage is divorce.

Couples will need to find groups and other couples to talk to who will show them that they are not alone. They need to know that other couples have similar behaviors, and that they are still accepted in spite of their worst behaviors. The shame diminishes when there is a network of couples providing the support necessary for the relationship to survive.

Sexual co-addicts must join the recovery process.

The co-addict is the person who marries the sex addict. Contrary to what many people may think, co-addicts don't become that way because of the sex addict. Marrying a sex addict is not an accident. The partners of sex addicts have chosen this relationship for good reasons. They may be abuse victims experiencing codependency and intimacy disorder. Some sexual co-addicts are bashful or inhibited about sex. They believe that if they marry a sex addict they will have a good sex life because they will never have to initiate—the sex addict always will.

Co-addicts may assume that when their sex addict gets into recovery all of their troubles will be over. They may think their problems have been due to the sexual acting out and when that stops all difficulties will stop. The problem is that they expect the sex addict to do all the work of recovery. It is vitally important for sexual co-addicts to look at themselves and not put all the pressure of recovery of the relationship on the sex addict. The co-addict will need to be in recovery too.

Sexually addicted couples must take mutual responsibility for the disease of their relationship.

When both members of a sexually addicted relationship can see their need to be in recovery, then they have accepted that they are mutually responsible for their relationship. This does not mean the co-addict is responsible for the behaviors of the sex addict. Neither does it mean the sex addict is responsible for the unhealthy or addictive behaviors of the co-addict. It does mean they both are responsible for the state of their relationship.

One trait of an unhealthy family is that partners blame each other and don't take responsibility for their own problems. Most conversations start with the words, "You always" or "You never." In healthy relationships, however, conversations begin with "I think" or "I feel" or "I take responsibility for the fact that . . ."

One exercise I recommend sexually addicted couples practice is called the "couple's personal inventory." At first on a daily basis and later on a weekly basis, couples should contract to take fifteen minutes by themselves and make two lists. One list is entitled, "The things that you did today (or this week) that were helpful to me or to our relationship." The second list is called, "The things that I did that were not helpful to you or to our relationship." When the two lists are compiled by each partner they should get together and exchange lists. They can ask questions of clarification, but they are *not* to add to each other's list. Comments like "You forgot that I . . ." or "You forgot when you . . ." are not allowed.

This exercise forces the couple to stop blaming each other, to take responsibility for their own behavior, to affirm their partner, and to start educating each other on what they like. If sexually addicted couples can accept mutual responsibility for the disease of the relationship then they can take the first step of Recovering Couples Anonymous. "*We* admitted that we are powerless over our relationship and that our life together had become unmanageable."

The co-addict must realize that he or she is not responsible for the sexual sobriety of the addict. Sex addicts are responsible for their own recovery and for setting their own boundaries. Questions like,

"Should you be watching that?" or "Should you be going to that place?" will only remind addicts of old behavior and memories. Sex addicts must be responsible for their own behaviors if they are to recover.

To build trust, sex addicts need to treat their spouse with consistency and caring. They should maintain trust by calling when they will be late, explaining any behavior that may seem questionable, and being considerate of their partner's feelings. One sex addict was watching his kids at the bowling alley when a woman approached him and struck up a conversation with him about bowling and the kids. When his wife discovered them talking together, she was enraged. Instead of accusing her of not trusting him, the man said, "I can see that this scene would remind you of my past behaviors. That must really hurt." He allowed her to have her feelings, and she felt heard, accepted, and cared for.

Sexually addicted couples will have to heal their image of the ideal relationship.

Almost all couples have an ideal of the perfect marriage. Sexually addicted couples will have to "bury," reclaim, or get help with some of their ideals because they have been violated over and over again or they were unrealistic in the first place. For example, almost all couples vow to be faithful to each other when they are married. Most sexually addicted couples have experienced major violations of this vow. Some couples expect to have a certain house, a certain type of family, or a certain amount of money in the bank. Either the addiction or circumstances or both have prevented attaining these.

Some sexually addicted couples have operated with unrealistic Christian images. One couple focused on the idea of never letting the sun set on their anger (Eph. 4:26). They would talk, argue, and fight into the middle of the night, long past sunset, trying to get things straight. The sex addict would not be satisfied until his wife had forgiven him, agreed with him, or made up. All the wife wanted was to escape, be by herself, and get away from his incessant talking and various demands.

I encourage sexually addicted couples to make a list defining the "ideal" couple: They never commit adultery, they have lots of money, their kids are perfect, and so on. Then the couple should ask themselves which items on the list they have violated. Before they get too down on themselves they should ask more questions.

First, which of the ideals on the list is realistic? Those that are not realistic should be discarded. For example, they might say, "We give ourselves permission not to have the best house in the neighborhood."

Second, which of the ideals can be restored? It is realistic to be sexually faithful in marriage. This is certainly a positive Christian value. Many of our sexually addicted couples renew their marriage vows, sometimes in the presence of a minister.

Finally, which of the ideals can be achieved with help? For example, a couple may want to attain financial stability and decide to consult a financial sponsor to help set budgets, suggest solutions, and help monitor progress.

Sexually addicted couples may never be the perfect couple they once imagined, but with help they can salvage their relationship, building a marriage of realistic goals and worthy ideals.

Sexually addicted couples must beware of reverting to old patterns of behavior.

A while back I was trying to correct one of my son's tennis swings. The correction allowed him to hit the ball harder and more accurately. He complained, however, that it felt "weird," and it hurt. Of course it did. It was unfamiliar, because he was using muscles in a new way. Later I discovered him practicing with someone else and hitting the ball the same old way. It didn't work as well, but it felt better.

Recovery is much the same. The new behaviors and healthy choices will work better and produce healthy results, but they "hurt." They don't feel familiar, they are scary, and they take lots of work. Recovery is hard work and is painful at times even though it produces joy and serenity and health.

Sexually addicted couples in recovery will experience new intimacy in their relationship, but it is unfamiliar. We are creatures of habit and of comfort. If we learned destructive patterns growing up, those are familiar, and we may unconsciously revert to them at times.

Sexually addicted couples must be aware of this temptation. What was normal for them may have been fighting, deception, adultery, silence, coldness, sexual unavailability, and endless other forms of craziness. Sometimes this craziness might seem more normal and safer than newer intimacies.

The early days of recovery when the couple experiences new honesty and relationship must be followed up with great discipline and care. Recovery is not a constantly wonderful progression. The old patterns will reoccur. This should not be interpreted as failure, but as a sign of the difficulty of the journey.

Sexually addicted couples should not expect social support for their recovery.

Just as recovery is unfamiliar for the couple, so it is for those around them. Families (even children), work associates, and old friends may not support the recovery process. They may not understand it or agree with it. They may not like the new honesty or changed behaviors because it makes them uncomfortable with their own way of living. And they may simply like things better the "old" way.

The result is that sexually addicted couples may encounter resistance to the changes they want to make. A brother of a sexual addict asked, "When are we going to be a normal family again?" The addict said, "Never! Normal is crazy." The brother was extremely angry and still hasn't talked to the addict.

One of our female alumni appeared on a TV show, and even though she wore a disguise, someone at church recognized her.

Eventually the pastor asked her to leave the church because her presence was causing too much tension in the "body of Christ."

Sexually addicted couples have to be strong in the face of misunderstanding, judgment, and hostility. They will have to establish new networks of support for themselves. Ultimately they might have to move, change jobs, or not see their families for a while. This will be very painful, but could be necessary to stay in recovery. The couple may need to grieve many relationships that they have lost.

Sexually addicted couples who don't work on this relationship will repeat the same mistakes in the next.

Sometimes the pain, shame, sadness, and anger is so intense for a sexually addicted couple that they think the only solution is to get divorced. They may think "I made a mistake and found the wrong partner. This is not the one that God *really* chose for me. I still need to find him or her." They think that with a new husband or wife all their problems will disappear.

One sexually addicted couple met each other after recovery. He was recovering from sexual addiction for five years, she from alcoholism for ten years. They assumed that since they were in recovery *individually* that their relationship would be easy. In the early days it was exciting and wonderful. However, several months into it the honeymoon wore off, and old issues from previous marriages returned. They asked themselves, "How could this new person be so much like my old partner?"

The reason is that they probably chose someone just like their old partner. They probably learned how to make this selection in their family of origin. Even though they were both in individual recovery their relationship experienced old problems. Healing of relationships needs to happen while a person is in a relationship. You can't practice relationship issues by yourself.

I am not arguing that a couple should stay married at all costs. As a Christian, I believe strongly in marriage, but not every marriage succeeds. If one person is getting beaten up physically or emotionally, they might need to get out. Even a sex addict might need to separate if the spouse can't get into recovery, forgive, and work on healing the relationship. However, realize that getting out of one relationship will not bring success in the next one. Many people have been married several times, and each marriage is a carbon copy of the last one.

Recovery for couples is a daily challenge, yet there is great hope of success. The wounds of the past will heal. With God's help and the support of others, couples can find new joy.

Sexually addicted couples should be considerate of their children.

One of the most frequent questions sexually addicted couples ask is, "What should we tell the children?" Depending on their age, the children should be told that Dad or Mom is getting help for sex addiction and that sex addiction is about not being able to stop sexual behaviors outside of marriage. Most of all, children need to know that Mom and Dad intend to stay together and that they, the children, will be safe. In early recovery parents should hold family meetings to let the children know in simple terms what is going on. Parents should explain the changes that will ensue, such as meetings the parents will have to attend, or having to move to a new location.

As they communicate to their children, sexually addicted couples need to model for children how to express their feelings. They should not tell their feelings so as to get sympathy or support from their children, for that would be emotional incest. The children should see, however, that their parents have feelings, are dealing with them, and are making healthier choices.

Most situations that I have known demonstrate that kids are extremely resilient and understanding if the parents are honest with them. Being frank about sexual sins gives the parents the chance to talk about sexual morality with credibility. They are being honest. They know what they are talking about. It also allows the children the chance to come to their parents when they are trying to make tough sexual choices.

Many sexually addicted couples recognize that they have harmed their children and look for ways to make amends. A parent may say, "I'm sorry that I have been angry with you lately. This anger is not your fault. And it doesn't mean I don't love you. I was working through some issues in my life and I took my anger about them out on you. I'll try not to do it again." The parent might also say, "If you ever feel I am doing something to you that is not fair, please come directly to me and we will talk about it."

In ways like this the parent teaches the children to take responsibility for behavior. The parent is also showing children that they are loved and that they don't deserve unfair treatment. As children learn to take responsibility, make healthy choices, and not allow themselves to be abused, the chain of addiction in a family system is broken.

Sexually addicted couples can grow together spiritually.

The greatest miracle of recovery is a deepening relationship with God. As sexual addicts grow individually, they must bring their spiritual growth to their partner and learn how to grow together spiritually as a couple. In early recovery the sexually addicted couple should establish a "spiritual quest" contract, pledging to go to church together, pray and read Scripture together, or have family devotions. Whatever the contract, it should be monitored by Christian friends, a support network, or the couple's pastor.

Couples must be aware that either partner could be a spiritual abuse victim. If so, participating in any religious practice may remind them of past pain. One sex addict was a minister's son who was sexually and emotionally abused by his father and who was forced to be at church many hours every week. All of these dynamics make it very hard for him to go into a church building. For years he was unable to tell his wife why he didn't want to go to church.

Without that information she believed that he didn't care, and her anger only drove him farther away from church.

A spiritual contract helps a couple to build trust. They commit to each other and to God to be honest and faithful to each other. Sometimes, to seal this vow, a couple will officially rededicate their marriage vows in a ceremony.

We live in a culture that has been, and continues to be, wounded by divorce and broken families. Sexually addicted couples who survive their pain and rebuild their marriages have much to teach us about the joys of becoming one flesh, breaking the cycle of abuse, and rebuilding families.

13.

Recovery for Congregations

I know a pastor whose predecessor was accused of having sex with a number of boys from his confirmation class. The new pastor described to me how much pain the congregation is experiencing because of this abuse. One of the victims even threatened to bomb the church.

In Wisconsin, an adult survivor of sexual abuse by a priest was arrested because he threatened to kill the priest. The man, not the priest, is in jail.

In Minneapolis, one attorney successfully sued pastors and churches for millions of dollars for the sexual damage they have done to child and adult victims.

In another state one of the members of the church council had affairs with fifteen married women in one of the adult Sunday school classes. Husbands are angry. The whole church is in shock. Members don't trust each other. Some are threatening to leave and start a new church.

Meanwhile, tremendous public attention has been focused on several well-known televangelists because of their sexual misconduct.

These are a few examples of the pain and grief that sexual misconduct by a pastor or church leader can create in the church. This chapter is about how sexual sin affects congregations and what we might do to heal these situations.

UNHEALTHY CHURCHES

We must begin by accepting the fact that many congregations are very unhealthy themselves.

Recently I was talking to a woman pastor who was directing a conference on the issue of pastors and sexual misconduct with members of their congregations. I asked if there would be workshops on how to get help for such pastors. She was surprised that I would ask such a question and said that the thought of dealing with perpetrators at the conference was enough to raise her blood pressure. After further discussion she said, "I guess we never considered the possibility of putting these pastors back together."

There is tremendous anger in the church about sexual sin. This anger leads to judgmental behavior, blaming, and a great deal of self-righteousness. All of these behaviors illustrate that the church at many levels is a dysfunctional family: They don't talk, don't feel, minimize, blame, and deny. Also remember the roles that a dysfunctional family plays: heroes, scapegoats, lost children, mascots, enablers, doers, saints, and little princesses and princes. Does your local church have people playing those roles?

Sex addicts are not the only people in a church who may be religiously addicted or codependent. I was about to speak to a group of pastors at a local church. Before the speech the host pastor came up to me and said, "I'm sorry the coffee isn't ready. I don't know how to make it and none of the women seem to be around." The women who make coffee at the church are not all codependents, but we must admit that many in the church depend on the doers, the enablers, the addicted, and the codependent to get things done. As another pastor said, "Without them, where would we be?"

In a dysfunctional church people don't get together to share fellowship but because they fear God. They don't talk about their problems, and since everyone wants to be liked, they will blame others for their problems. Worst of all, as a dysfunctional unit, it carries with it the potential for profoundly abusing its parishioners emotionally, spiritually, and even sexually.

I am aware of churches, for example, in which pastors have

been sexual with up to sixty of their people. One such pastor remained in his pulpit for twenty-five years! The victims said nothing, others who knew said nothing, and of course, the pastor said nothing. Imagine the individual and collective pain that people endured in that church for twenty-five years. Yet many members of the community thought this pastor was an ideal public figure and that this church was the ideal church.

Dysfunctional churches are not places of healing. If the church is to offer help for sexual addiction it too must begin with Christ's commandment, "Love others as you love yourself." The church must heal itself if it is going to heal others.

Traditionally, the church has followed the don't-talk rule, thinking that it was the most caring thing to do. It has not wanted to permanently ruin anyone's reputation by making the situation public. Victims, in many cases, have felt ignored. The church has further harmed them by not taking their problems and long-lasting harm more seriously. Recently many victims have turned to the legal system to make the point of how seriously they have been hurt. Many of the victims that I know are not interested in money from lawsuits; they are interested in justice.

Regardless of the legal implications of abuse, the church must now begin to grapple openly with the issue of sexual abuse within the church. We can no longer hide behind the no-talk rule. We must do something about the problem.

If we are to heal the wounds of the congregation, we must bring healing to two groups of victims. Those who have had direct sexual involvement with pastors or church leaders are *primary victims*. Others whose trust in the pastor or church leader has been betrayed are *secondary victims*.

PRIMARY VICTIMS

Primary victims have been sexually harassed, sexually teased, touched inappropriately, told sexual jokes, or had a sexual relationship with pastors or church leaders. As a result, the victim is wounded by the sexual activity and needs help. There are several actions that the church can take:

1. *Advocates.* Victims may not recognize that they are victims. Just like incest victims or other abuse victims, they may assume responsibility and feel guilty for the sexual activity. They may think it is not that important of an event. They may have reasons why they don't want others, including their families, to know about it. In some extremely abusive and painful situations, they may not remember the event.

As victims begin to recognize the pain they will need advocates to help them process their healing. It is the advocate's job to assure that the victim is heard and believed. It is also their job to assure that the victim gets counseling. The advocate may accompany the victim to meetings with church leaders and help the victim to state the facts. The advocate will take note of the response of the church and make sure that the victim understands and hears it. The advocate may help the victim state the need for counseling and for financial assistance in getting it.

An advocate can be a counselor, lawyer, or concerned person. A number of denominations are currently training people to function in this role.

Advocates may be the first ones to whom victims tell details about their abuse. Advocates should be trained in the protective procedures to follow, particularly if the victim is a minor. Victims will need to know they are safe and that there is help available. They may not have the strength to pursue this on their own.

2. *Believing.* The most critical element in the process, at least initially, is that the victims are believed. There are cases in which victims are not telling the whole truth. Researchers have found that these are relatively rare. Remember that what is being told is the victim's *perception* of the facts. Even if that perception is not entirely true, it may be very real to the victim. Victims need to hear that their report and perceptions are accepted and that they will get help.

A church or a denomination will need to investigate all reports of sexual misconduct. While this is going on they need to keep victims and their advocates informed of the process. Communication needs to be truthful and prompt. Many victims report that their phone calls are not returned or that they are ignored. It will not always be the job of church officials to be the ones to listen to victims, but they can let them know they understand how hurtful the experience has been.

Being believed allows victims to feel *safe*. Their hurt has been heard and accepted. By believing the church is also able to say that it will try not to let it happen again, that it takes the situation seriously, and that it will do something about it.

Being believed may be a new experience for victims. It didn't happen in their families and it hasn't happened much historically. Their advocates and others may need to continue to reinforce the fact that they are believed. Ultimately, the feeling of being believed leads to a sense of peace and perhaps a sense of justice.

3. *Fellowship.* During the initial process of getting help it is very important for the church to offer fellowship to victims. If the facts of the situation are known locally, victims may feel extremely uneasy participating in their local church, and perhaps in *any* church. The church will need to be considerate of the victims, letting them know that they are welcome at their own time and comfort level to come back to church, or that the church will help them find another church in which they feel more comfortable.

4. *Providing Counseling.* This is perhaps the most important of all initial considerations. Victims with the help of their advocate must find counseling support. This can be individual therapy, a counseling group, or both. Some cities have support and counseling groups for victims of pastoral sexual abuse. Many counseling agencies have counselors who specialize in this kind of problem.

Because of the nature of this situation, the counselor should not be a pastoral counselor because there may be too much negative identification with this role. The counselor may also need to be the same sex as the victim.

The church should offer to pay for this counseling even if the victim has insurance or the financial ability to do so. In this way the church says to the victim that it understands and accepts responsibility for the harm done.

In counseling the victim, the counselor should not focus only on the abuse at hand, but also deal with any earlier abuse suffered at the hands of family or church. Counseling that deals only with the current situation will keep the victim stuck in early phases of healing.

At some point in the counseling process, victims need to move from being victims to being "survivors." Survivors are those whose lives are not controlled by or oriented around the pain of the abuse. There are stages to pass through to get to this place:

There is *knowledge* of the abuse, past and present, and *acceptance* of that knowledge. Knowledge may come slowly. Memories, perhaps extremely painful, are sometimes not readily available to the conscious mind. Victims who are in therapy may require months, if not years, to recall all events. Acceptance means that what is remembered is accepted as being abusive. Acceptance may require that the victim *confront* the abuser. If the abuser is no longer around or alive, it may be that just telling others, including those in the church, can be confrontation enough.

Anger about the abuse must be expressed in a constructive manner. Many victims get stuck in anger, feeling that if they stay angry enough, they won't be hurt again. However, being angry traps them in the role of victim.

Survivors know that they have power over their own lives. They have the ability to set boundaries, to say no, and to take care of themselves. Survivors are able to get on with their life and work on other issues as they need to. Their recovery may take years, but their peace and serenity will grow daily.

5. *Reconciliation.* Victims of pastoral sexual abuse may need to be outside of the church for a while. It is important for Christians not to see this time as a spiritual failure, but as a time of healing for the victim.

If victims experience the patience of the church, they will want to come back and be reconciled. If they were partially at fault, survivors may want to admit their part in the affair and ask the forgiveness of the church. Or, in rare cases, they may want to confront and forgive their abuser. Any confrontation of this nature should be done in the presence of a counselor. I have had the privilege of participating in one of these confrontations. It was one of the most powerful healing sessions I have ever seen.

6. *Preventive education.* The whole church needs education about the nature of abuse, beginning with the earliest ages in Sunday school. It can be very much like the education we give children about abuse in school. I envision a time when both pastors who have abused and survivors who have been abused can tell their stories to churches. This could be educational in helping people know what dangerous situations to look for and avoid, and how to establish healthy boundaries for themselves. Any education of this kind should include lots of advice about how and where to get help.

SECONDARY VICTIMS

Secondary victims are members of the congregation who placed their spiritual trust and confidence in the pastor or leader. Secondary victims can also be members of the local public community who knew the pastor or church leader. The strength of their faith may rest with the witness and example of this pastor. When that is betrayed by inappropriate, sinful sexual activity of any kind, there can be a massive injury to the person's ability to trust, including in God.

When the pastor sins sexually, some might tell church members, "Put your faith in God, not in this pastor." Others might say, "Forgive and forget. That is the Christian thing to do." If we are to offer healing from the wounds of sexual misconduct we must break with tradition. Most of all we must be honest with each other. Here are some strategies to heal the wounds of sexual sin in the church:

Breaking the Silence: "We *Do* Talk, We *Don't* Deny or Minimize"

I met with a group of people from a church who were extremely angry about how the sexual misconduct of a former pastor had been handled. The pastor had been abusing young boys, and the leaders of the church who knew of the abuse sent him to treatment without informing the congregation. Later, the pastor went on to a new church without saying good-bye at the old church. Seven years later one of his victims sued him. Only when the news hit the paper did members of the congregation know what had really happened. Upon hearing the real story, members of this group were furious with the pastor and with the church officials who hadn't told them the truth.

In this case, the congregation should have been told because there may have been other abuse victims needing help. But there are other reasons for breaking the silence. The rumors that circulated in this congregation were dividing the congregation. People were taking sides in the debate over what really happened. The congregation was ashamed, thinking it was their fault that the pastor left.

If the truth had been told it would have been shocking and painful. However, all of the things the church avoided eventually happened anyway, and with deeper hurt and anger. This congregation was victimized twice, once by their pastor and once by their church officials. By avoiding the consequences, the church prevented both the pastor and the congregation from getting real help.

Breaking the silence means telling the truth. The first Sunday after the facts become known and are verified, an appropriate leader must tell the people the general nature of the facts. The sermon or Bible teaching that Sunday should be specific to sexual sin. I highly recommend the stories of David, Samson, the woman caught in adultery, or the Samaritan woman at the well. These stories remind us that there are sexual sinners in the Bible, but with confrontation and consequences come healing.

Church members should be encouraged to talk about their feelings of hurt, betrayal, and anger, but they should not gossip about the specific details or speculate about who was involved with the pastor.

Members should be informed about what is going to happen to the pastor. Later they should be given updates. The pastor should not be allowed to disappear, never to be heard from again. Instead, the church should set up meetings to allow people to come together and talk about what happened. One congregation conducted a series of three public meetings. In the first the church's lawyer came to explain the legal situation as the pastor and the denomination had been sued by various victims. In the second meeting people broke up into small groups and freely discussed their feelings about the situation. In the final meeting a pastor from the national church came to hear the feelings of the congregation as expressed by the representatives of these small groups. He then conducted a healing service in the sanctuary of the church.

Not all members of a church will attend such meetings. Some will not want to face the issues. That is certainly their choice. We should never force anyone to talk about feelings. That in itself might be abusive. The public meetings that take place should be elective for those who want to come.

Some church members will be very angry. This could be extremely divisive to the church. Public meetings should be conducted with very clear boundaries about acceptable language and conduct. These meetings are for people to express their personal feelings, not to blame or judge others. The expression of anger is certainly acceptable, but it can be done in a constructive way.

Other church members will have doubts about their faith as a result of the sexual misconduct of their pastor. We should allow them the freedom to be honest about this. Instead of judging them for their lack of faith, we should remember that Job and many other people of faith had struggles and doubts in difficult situations.

The pastor who replaces the abusive pastor will need to be prepared for lots of counseling and small group sharing outside of these meetings. This new pastor will need the patience of Job. This pastor should be a good listener and accept that many of their feelings will be difficult.

Breaking the silence also means that the church will announce that it is providing help for both primary and secondary victims. It will tell people how to obtain counseling, how to contact an advocate, or how to get financial help for recovery.

Another strong possibility is that there may be people in the church who have been victimized by other pastors, parents, or others. The sexual misconduct of the current pastor may bring these memories to the surface. Again, counseling resources should be provided.

Breaking the silence also involves education about sexual addiction. This is important to inform people about the nature of the disease and how it operates. Such information might help people understand the dynamics of the sinful behavior that took place. We must accept that there will be those in the congregation who will be hiding their own private sexually addicted lives. If we gently educate the congregation about this disease and inform people about the help that is available, this can lead many to healing. I can not emphasize enough the quality of gentleness. Sex addicts already have felt enough shame to last them several lifetimes. Judging these behaviors harshly will only increase their shame and force them deeper into hiding.

Grieving: "We *Do* Feel"

There are definite stages of grief that a congregation will need to experience in order to heal. I am borrowing a system for understanding grief from Dr. Glen W. Davidson, who years ago studied the process of feelings that mothers went through who had lost children. The four categories that he discovered with mothers apply very well to all grief situations.

1. *Shock and numbness.* When a pastor or church leader sins sexually, it is a shock. It is hard to believe. It is difficult to accept. In some cases, the pain may be so intense the mind takes over and shuts feelings down. Without this protective measure the pain might be unbearable.

The danger of this phase is that it appears that people are coping "nicely." A congregation that thinks it is doing nicely and holding up courageously will not know what to do with painful feelings when they surface weeks or months later. People might ask themselves, "Does this mean that I am not a good Christian?" Not wanting to seem immature, they will have a hard time admitting to the feelings. As a result they bury their feelings only to have them surface, perhaps even years later.

2. *Searching and yearning.* Sometimes when we lose a loved one we wish they were back. We search for them. We refuse to clean the rooms of those who died, thinking they might return. In the same way, congregations may search and yearn for their pastor or their image of the pastor to return. They may be very quick to forgive and want the pastor to stay. They may create elaborate fantasies about how it couldn't have happened.

One pastor of a church had at least ten sexual relationships with young boys. A woman in the church refused to believe it had happened even though the pastor went to jail. In her eyes the boys, their parents, the media, and the prosecuting attorney were wrong about the facts. This is searching and yearning for the pastor to be back.

This phase can also be one of intense anger. When a loved one dies we are sometimes angry that he *deserted* us. Since the pastor is still alive, the anger may get displaced onto various others. Denominational or church leaders may be blamed for taking the pastor away. The media or lawyers are often targets. Certainly, many victims get blamed for "taking the pastor away from us."

3. *Disorientation.* When we lose a loved one we don't know what to do without them. They provided many necessary functions. We have all known widows, for example, whose husbands protected them from all sorts of things like driving or paying bills. When the husband dies the widow is left helpless to do basic things.

When a pastor leaves there can also be this physical and emotional disorientation. The pastor probably provided many physical functions for the church and certainly offered emotional support to lots of people. I once heard a man remark, "He didn't know how much I relied on him to just get through each day."

Beyond this, the pastor's leaving creates a *spiritual* disorientation. People will not know how to relate to God, how to interpret Scripture, how to lead worship, or how to pray.

Some people may feel angry at this stage, but most will feel anxious. They will worry about who will conduct the upcoming services, or they will feel a deep dread about something terrible happening. People may simply be afraid to come to church or more deeply anxious about life in general. People may find themselves irritable about little things that don't seem related to the church or to the pastor.

Anxiety and anger left unexpressed lead to depression. The whole congregation may seem to be down. The mood is low. Worship is not positive. No joy is present. Individual members may be personally depressed. If the power of the loss of the pastor is not recognized as a factor in their lives, they may become frightened by their depression. It will seem to come from nowhere, with no explanation. They will be baffled and frightened.

4. *Reorganization.* After the congregation has moved through the other phases and expressed their hurts, they will come to a period of reorganization, where they accept the situation and move on. Reorganization means that the congregation finds or accepts a new pastor. New and creative solutions are found for the problems the pastor used to solve.

The stages of grief just described take various lengths of time to work through. The whole process, if accomplished in a healthy way, will take a year or two. This sounds like a long time, and it is. People will get impatient with it. If enough time is not taken, however, feelings will stay buried, fester, and cause anger and resentments later on.

Reconciliation: "We *Don't* Blame"

A congregation that wants to heal will not allow itself to blame others for the problems in the church. Instead it will offer understanding and help to those most affected by the sexual sins of its pastors and members.

Victims will need to feel welcome at church. Families of the victims and the pastor will need to be embraced. Pastors, if they are in recovery and humble, will need to be restored to the church. This does not mean they should be restored to pastoral duties, but there might be a time and a place when they are allowed to publicly apologize for their behaviors. Their apology might include a humble acceptance of sinful behavior, an admission of wrong-doing, and an acknowledgment of how painful and destructive the behaviors were. This could be healing for both the pastor, the church, and any victims.

Reconciliation may need to take place between the church and the pastor's family. Although the family did not cause the problem, their presence in the church may be a painful reminder of the situation. Instead of ignoring the family, the church should be sensitive to their needs. If the pastor and his family have left, the family might be invited back at least to say good-bye. This will allow everyone to feel a sense of closure to the situation.

In my experience another person who may need reconciliation is the pastor who immediately replaces the one who has left. This pastor, who faces enormous difficulties, will need to be an exceptionally strong and mature Christian and will need much support. In the Twin Cities we now have a support group for pastors in these situations. Reconciliation in the church means that the members accept the difficulties the new pastor faces and are willing to support the pastor in every way possible.

Prevention: "We *Do* Have Boundaries"

Unhealthy boundaries typify an unhealthy congregation. In such congregations emotional incest, spiritual mind rape, spiritual invasiveness, abandonment, and all other forms of abuse can take place.

A healthy church is one in which boundaries are respected. Members respect themselves and each other. Members take care of themselves and allow others to do the same. Members work to not injure others emotionally, physically, sexually, and spiritually.

Even Jesus established boundaries for himself. He went into the wilderness to be by himself. He got into a boat and went to the other side of the sea when the crowds got too demanding. Rather than chasing after people to get them to believe his message, he told the truth and allowed it to sink in. And he did everything with love.

To begin the process of changing a church from one with unhealthy boundaries to one with healthy ones, we must educate the church about boundaries: how they can be invaded and how much damage such invasion can do. Next, church leaders should *model* healthy boundaries. They should not respond to every demand of the congregation. And they should not take advantage of others, either. By modeling healthy boundaries, church leaders can show the congregation how to care for themselves and others.

Healing the wounds of a congregation that has been affected by sexual sinfulness is a long process that will be painful. In this pain, however, we can be truly vulnerable with each other about our feelings. Vulnerability leads to intimacy and to profound spiritual friendship. In all things, God *will* work for good with those that love him. This is the hope of salvation for the whole body of Christ.

Conclusion

The inevitable final question is, "Can sexual addiction be cured?" The answer depends on how you define the word *cure*. In the case of sexual addiction, many Christians would like the word *cure* to mean a permanent removal of all the disease. They would like to think that salvation, faith, and prayer would eradicate all sexual temptation and the urge to commit sexual sin.

However, there is no foolproof cure for sexual addiction. Recovering addicts may have stopped acting out, but they know that they are always at risk to act out again. Therefore they must be continually careful about maintaining their program, going to meetings, and avoiding "slippery" places where temptation lurks.

As a diabetic, I battle a disease that has no cure. I can manage it, live with it, effectively treat all of the symptoms, but I cannot get rid of it. There is no permanent cure for diabetes.

The same is true for my sexual addiction: It also has no permanent cure. But the recovery process does offer me and many others healing—an ongoing process of improvement. Lives will get better, the pain of abuse will diminish, feelings will improve, relationships will become more intimate, marriages will get stronger, and sexual temptation will decrease. This is a healing process, but it is *not* a cure.

Like Paul, sexual addicts must deal with their "thorn in the flesh":

> To keep me from becoming conceited because of these surpassingly great revelations, there was given me a thorn in my flesh, a messenger of Satan, to torment me. Three times I pleaded with the Lord to take it away from me. But he said to me, "My grace is sufficient for you, for my power is made perfect in weakness." Therefore I will boast all the more gladly about my weaknesses, so that Christ's power may rest on me. That is why, for Christ's sake, I delight in weaknesses, in insults, in hardships, in persecutions, in difficulties. For when I am weak, then I am strong. (2 Cor. 12:7–10)

Sex addicts are capable of great spiritual healing, of profound relationship to God, even though their sexual addiction may not be "cured." The fact that they accept their powerlessness over their disease leaves them with a great humility and need for God, which is a deep aspect of their spiritual healing. Like Paul, their ongoing "thorn in the flesh" allows them to point to their weakness as individuals and their need for salvation from God.

Ultimately, if all things are possible with God, we can accept that there are sex addicts who may be cured. For them sexual temptation may never again be a problem. For most, however, this won't happen. Yet, even in the lack of cure there can be great spiritual healing, healing that can be a wonderful witness to the entire Christian community.

This book has been written not to be the final answer to the problem of sexual addiction, but rather to provide information to educate the church. Education gets people talking, and educated talking starts the process of healing.

There is an old Alcoholics Anonymous expression that is used at the end of meetings: "Take what you like and leave the rest." In the course of reading this book you may have disagreed with me several times. Yet it is my hope that you will take what this book has to offer and, even though you may disagree with certain points, use it to stimulate you to think, pray, and act. If you are hurting as a result of sexual addiction, don't try to process the hurt yourself. Talk to someone, get some help, work together with others. While sexual sin is devastating, there is still hope for healing.

When Jesus became a man he suffered our fate as human beings. He was humiliated, tortured, and killed. Paul writes that Jesus, "being found in appearance as a man . . . humbled himself and became obedient to death" (Phil. 2:8). Sexual addicts also must be obedient unto death—death of their old addictive lifestyle.

Yet Jesus, after dying, rose again. After dying to themselves, sexual addicts also can live again. They can experience freedom, spiritual resurrection, and peace. When they allow Jesus to step into the deepest shadow of their most secret sins, he will flood that place with redeeming light.

I wish I could describe to you the testimony of hundreds of sex addicts who have gone through this process of death and rebirth. Lives have been restored, marriages healed, and families strengthened. Careers and economic situations have been rebuilt. Best of all, the recovering sexual addict experiences a deep sense of the presence and redeeming grace of God.

There *is* hope for the sexual addict. If you are one, my prayer is that you will find this hope. You have been wounded and lonely all your life. You don't have to stay that way. There is peace. May you find that peace now.

Notes

CHAPTER THREE

[1]Gerald Blanchard, *Sex Offender Treatment: A Psychoeducational Model* (Golden Valley, Minn.: Institute for Behavioral Medicine, 1988).

CHAPTER FOUR

[1]Patrick Carnes, *Don't Call It Love* (New York: Bantam Books, 1991).
[2]Ibid.
[3]Craig Nakken, *The Addictive Personality* (Center City, Minn.: Hazelden, 1988).

CHAPTER FIVE

The ideas in this chapter were originally published as an article, "Sexual Addiction and Clergy," *Pastoral Psychology* 39, no. 4 (March 1991): 213–35.
[1]"How Common Is Pastoral Indiscretion?" *Leadership* 11, no. 1 (Winter 1988): 12–13.
[2]Tim LaHaye, *If Ministers Fall, Can They Be Restored?* (Grand Rapids: Zondervan, 1990).
[3]Peter Rutter, *Sex in the Forbidden Zone* (Los Angeles: Jeremy P. Tarcher, 1989).

CHAPTER SIX

[1]John and Linda Friel, *The Secrets of Dysfunctional Families* (Deerfield Beach, Fla.: Health Communications, Inc., 1988).

CHAPTER SEVEN

[1]Patrick Carnes, *Don't Call It Love* (New York: Bantam Books, 1991).

[2]Patricia Love, *The Emotional Incest Syndrome* (New York: Bantam Books, 1990).

[3]Patrick Carnes, *Don't Call It Love* (New York: Bantam Books, 1991).

[4]John Bradshaw, *Healing the Shame that Binds You* (Deerfield Beach, Fla.: Health Communications, Inc., 1988).

[5]Sandra Wilson, *Released from Shame* (Downers Grove, Ill.: InterVarsity, 1990).

[6]Patrick Carnes, *Out of the Shadows* (Minneapolis: CompCare Pubs., 1983).

CHAPTER EIGHT

[1]Harvey Milkman and Stanley Sunderwirth, *Craving for Ecstasy* (Lexington, Mass.: D.C. Health and Co., 1987).

[2]Patrick Carnes, *Don't Call It Love* (New York: Bantam Books, 1991). *

CHAPTER NINE

[1]Other books on sexual addiction include Patrick Carnes, *Contrary to Love* (Minneapolis: CompCare Pubs., 1989); Ralph Earle and Gregory Crow, *Lonely All the Time* (New York: Pocket Books, 1989); and Ernest Kurtz, *Not-God* (Center City, Minn.: Hazelden, 1979).

CHAPTER ELEVEN

[1]Joyce and Clifford Penner, *The Gift of Sex* (Waco, Tex.: Word, 1981).

CHAPTER TWELVE

[1]Patrick Carnes, *Don't Call It Love* (New York: Bantam Books, 1991).

Resources

The following resources are not exhaustive. They are provided as beginning places to obtain help. Once you have decided to get help, you have overcome a major obstacle: you have decided that you can't do it alone and that you need God's help. Call or write, and don't be afraid to try more than one place until you find the help you need and feel comfortable with.

TWELVE-STEP FELLOWSHIPS FOR SEX ADDICTION

Each of these fellowships may have meetings in your town. Call them either to receive meeting information or to find contacts in your area. Each fellowship will vary slightly in their meeting formats or philosophy. One main difference might be how sobriety is defined. For example, Sexaholics Anonymous (SA) has, at least historically, had the strictest definition and the one that most Christians would be the most comfortable with. SA says that sobriety is sexual abstinence from any sexual activity except with one's spouse. However, even these distinctions might vary from town to town, as each meeting is a locally autonomous fellowship.

Sex Addicts Anonymous (SAA)
P.O. Box 3038
Minneapolis, MN 55403
(612) 871-1520, 339-0217

Sex and Love Addicts Anonymous (SLAA)
P.O. Box 119
New Town Branch
Boston, MA 02258
(617) 332-1845

Sexaholics Anonymous (SA)
P.O. Box 300
Simi Valley, CA 93062
(805) 581-3343

Sexual Compulsives Anonymous

East:
P.O. Box 1585
Old Chelsea Station
New York, NY 10011
(212) 340-8985

West:
4391 Sunset Boulevard
Suite 520
Los Angeles, CA 90029
(213) 859-5585

These fellowships have either developed their own resources or have recommended resource materials such as meeting directories, meeting formats, starter packets, big books, guides and answers to basic questions, and meditation books. Contact them and request ordering information.

The National Council on Sexual Addiction (NCSA) also provides resources and referrals.

National Council on Sexual Addiction
P.O. Box 20249
Wickenburg, AR 85358
(602) 684-7919

Big books or meditation books on sex addiction may be available at your local bookstore. Try these:

Hope and Recovery, published by CompCare in 1987, contains resource material and stories of recovering sex addicts.

Answers in the Heart, published by Harper and Row, is a meditation book written by sex addicts.

Out of the Shadows, Contrary to Love, and *Don't Call it Love,* all by Patrick Carnes, are the classic books on sex addiction. Carnes has also published a workbook to help addicts work through the twelve steps: *A Gentle Path Through the 12 Steps.* It contains helpful writing exercises.

Women, Sex, and Addiction by Charlotte Kasl is, as the title suggests, about women and sex addiction.

Lonely All the Time by Ralph Earle is enjoyable reading.

TWELVE-STEP FELLOWSHIPS FOR CO-SEX ADDICTION

The following are groups for spouses, partners, relatives, or friends of sex addicts. As the reader will note, each of the sex addict fellowships has a counterpart group for those who are sometimes referred to as "significant others."

CoSA National Service Organization
P.O. Box 1457
Minneapolis, MN 55414

S-ANON International Family Groups
P.O. Box 5117
Sherman Oaks, CA 91413
(818) 990-6910

Co-dependents of Sex and Love Addicts Anonymous (CO-SLAA)
P.O Box 614
Brookline, MA 02146-9998

SCA-ANON
East:
P.O. Box 1585
Old Chelsea Station
New York, NY 10011
West:
4391 Sunset Boulevard
Suite 520
Los Angeles, CA 90029

Like the sex addiction fellowships, these groups will have their own materials available.

Jennifer Schneider, M.D., has been an unofficial spokesperson of co-sex addicts. Her book, *Back from Betrayal,* published by Hazelden, describes the concerns of a spouse betrayed by sexual addiction.

There is a vast array of books on codependency. Melody Beattie has been the pioneer in the field. Her classic work is *Co-dependent No More.*

Two Christian authors have given us good material. I have come to know Nancy Groom and respect her books highly. Her three books are *Authority and Submission—A New Way of Looking at It, From Bondage to Bonding,* and *Married Without Masks.* Margaret Josephson Rinck's classic Christian book on codependency is *Can Christians Love Too Much?*

TWELVE-STEP FELLOWSHIPS FOR COUPLES

Recovering Couples Anonymous (RCA) is a relatively new fellowship (founded in 1988) for couples. It is not specifically for sexually addicted couples. Members seek to work the twelve steps in their relationship. The first step of RCA is "*We* admitted that we were powerless over our relationship and that our life together had become unmanageable." Since it is so new, there are fewer fellowships. The reader may have to write for information about starting a fellowship.

RCA
P.O. Box 27617
Golden Valley, MN 55422
(612) 473-3752

RCA is in the early days of developing its own materials. There is a short version of a big book available.

Jennifer Schneider and her husband, Bert, have been doing research with sexually addicted couples. Their new book is helpful: *Sex, Lies, and Forgiveness*.

Another book that I find insightful is Harville Hendrix's *Getting the Love You Want*.

Joyce and Clifford Penner have been helpful to Christian couples about sexual issues. See their book, *The Gift of Sex*.

CHRISTIAN TWELVE-STEP FELLOWSHIPS

Christians are beginning to form their own fellowships based on the Twelve Steps and with more intentional Christian language. The one that I know and trust the best is called Overcomers Outreach. They currently have over 800 fellowships around the country. For the most part these groups, like RCA, do not specifically address any particular addiction. Addicts who are recovering from any addictive substance or behavior are welcome to come. Several Overcomers groups may be for sex addicts only.

Overcomers Outreach
2290 W. Whittier Blvd., Suite D
LaHabra, CA 90631
(213) 697-3994

Rev. Vern Bittner was one of the first persons to write about the Twelve Steps in Christian language. His books, particularly *The 12 Steps for Christian Living,* are helpful guides to working the steps as Christians. Vern also heads an organization that helps churches start Twelve-Step groups for Christian living.

Recovery Publications has put out a helpful guide to working the steps called *The Twelve Steps—A Spiritual Journey.* It includes scriptural references and writing exercises.

FINDING COUNSELING

The reader may want to consult with or start a counseling relationship with a local doctor, psychiatrist, therapist, or pastor.

Golden Valley Health Center remains the best source of local referral information. The first treatment center for sexual addiction, Golden Valley over the last several years has trained, through its Institute, hundreds of caregivers in the basics of counseling sexual addicts. Based on its experience, it has compiled a list of counselors, counseling centers, and hospitals trained and equipped to deal with sexual addiction. You can call confidentially (and anonymously) to receive information about your area.

Golden Valley Health Center
4101 Golden Valley Rd.
Golden Valley, MN 55422
(800) 321-2273

Golden Valley has not compiled a list specific to Christian counselors. Many may be on their list, but some may not. If you are interested in a Christian counselor, several organizations may be able to help you with local referrals.

The Christian Association for Psychological Studies (CAPS) includes many Christian therapists. You may write to CAPS for referral to one of them. Their address is:

CAPS
P.O. Box 890279
Temecula, CA 92589

Rapha Hospital Treatment Centers are a network of counseling and treatment facilities that provide Christian care. They have a referral network available. Call 1-800-383-HOPE.

The Minirth-Meier Clinics are Christian centers that have developed addiction treatments. Call them at 1-800-229-3000.

A group called The Recovery Partnership, directed by Dr. Dale S. Ryan, is developing resources to help Christians and churches use recovery.

The Recovery Partnership
P.O. Box 11095
Whittier, CA 90603
(310) 857-6200

Many Christian organizations and denominations will have their own trusted counseling referrals. Call the ones that you know and trust. Or consult your pastor for information about a local counseling resource.

When you are "checking out" a counselor, interview him or her about their knowledge of sexual addiction and acceptance of it as a disease. If you seem to know more than they do as a result of reading this book, find someone else.

OTHER HELPFUL BOOKS

You will find the following books helpful. Many publishers are now producing helpful recovery-oriented books in these areas.

Families

John Bradshaw, *Bradshaw: On the Family*.
John and Linda Friel, *Adult Children—The Secrets of Dysfunctional Families*.
Virginia Satir, *Peoplemaking*.
Patricia Love, *The Emotional Incest Syndrome*.

Shame

John Bradshaw, *Healing the Shame that Binds You*.
Marilyn Mason and Merle Fossum, *Facing Shame*.
Sandra Wilson, *Released from Shame*.

Addiction

Craig Nakken, *The Addictive Personality*.
Gerald May, *Addiction and Grace*.

Ministry and Sexuality

Marie Fortune, *Is Nothing Sacred?*
Peter Rutter, *Sex in the Forbidden Zone*.
Tim LaHaye, *If Ministers Fall, Can They Be Restored?*
Lloyd Reddiger, *Sexual Ethics in Ministry*

Religious Addiction

Leo Booth, *Breaking the Chains*.
Jack Felton and Steve Arteburn, *Toxic Faith*.

Unhealthy Congregations

Anne Wilson Schaef, *The Addicted Organization*.

Remember that you can never heal yourself just by reading a book. Use them only as aids in your journey. There is never a better substitute than talking to someone.